Wicked GRAND RAPIDS

AMBERROSE HAMMOND

Charleston London

THE
History
PRESS

Published by The History Press
Charleston, SC 29403
www.historypress.net

Cover images: Policemen and detective images courtesy of Grand Rapids Public Library.

First published 2014

Manufactured in the United States

ISBN 978.1.62619.296.6

Library of Congress CIP data applied for.

For Tom.
Thank you for thirteen awesome years of friendship.
You are terribly missed. Look out for us "good guys" over here while
you are on the other side.

Contents

Acknowledgements

I'd like to thank Ruth from the Grand Rapids Public Library for helping me find photos and old newspaper articles. She was an immense help! Thank you as well to Tobin Buhk, fellow History Press author, for lending me some of his photos for inclusion in the book and helping me touch up old pictures; my commissioning editor, Greg Dumais, for having patience with me; David Schock, PhD, for his research and films on the Mina Dekker case and his website "Delayed Justice," which was very valuable; Carl Bajema's extensive collection of newspaper clippings—his work has been helpful on many of my research projects; Julie Williams for listening again…and again; Jeanette Weiden, who is always ready to help with her awesome genealogy skills; and last, to my mother, grandparents and friends, who are all very supportive of my 101 hobbies.

Introduction

I'm a lover of all things strange, creepy and unusual in Michigan's past and present. I especially have a love of reading old Michigan newspapers. It's like taking a trip back in time. You can read what was happening on any given day and learn what people were worried and concerned about, what products they were buying and what was making headlines. Once upon a time, you had to spend hours and hours sitting behind a microfilm reader in the corner of a library, getting dizzy as the old newspaper images whirled past you while you tried to locate an exact date. It was daunting, and unless you combed through the papers day by day, there was no way to randomly search through them for stories or specific topics. However, thanks to the digitization process, newspapers from communities small and large are being preserved digitally and made searchable in databases, helping to unearth forgotten local history that sat rolled up on film for decades in drawers, begging to be let out. Newspapers recorded the day-to-day lives of our ancestors. They are an excellent way to learn about a community's past and how far it has come.

I've always been intrigued by old crime, and through my research over the years and old newspaper obsession, I started to build up quite the collection of old, forgotten stories full of bandits, rogues, unscrupulous killers and unsolved murders. When I started to delve into many of the Grand Rapids papers, I discovered the Furniture City was in no short supply of wild, colorful and exciting old tales of murder and mayhem.

Before I started this project, I was talking with an editor at The History Press, and he worded the purpose of the "Wicked" book series in a way

$25 REWARD!

Dr. Fred Schermerhorn;

32 years old, 5 ft. 9 in. in height; weight about 170 pounds; light complexion, sandy mustache, heavy eyebrows extending quite across forehead; forehead very high; very full under eyes, and is a Spiritual Medium. Left Grand Rapids, Mich., on night of December 2, 1888, via C. & W. M. R. R. I will pay reward of **$25** for his discovery and detention.

LOOMIS K. BISHOP,
Sheriff of Kent County, Mich.

Left: An old "wanted" poster from Grand Rapids, 1888. *Courtesy of Tobin Buhk.*

Below: An antique postcard of Monroe Street. *Author's collection.*

I couldn't stop thinking about. He described the books as "untold stories about the sinister side of life in an area...that for better or worse helped shape the community." As I researched and wrote these stories for *Wicked Grand Rapids*, this statement was always in the back of my mind. Many of the stories in this book did, in fact, shape the community "for better or worse."

I wouldn't wish the fate of these stories on anyone, but I do hope you enjoy reading these lost and forgotten chapters of history from Grand Rapids' "wicked" past.

Chapter 1

Mail-Order Murder

James Allen was just one of many aliases Scott Mausell went by in his pursuit of money by lying to and stealing from old and widowed women who were looking for husbands. Older and feeble himself, Scott didn't want to end up back at a poor farm, where his wife, Eliza, had left him. After he had suffered a stroke that caused temporary paralysis, she wasn't able to care for him and went to live with her brother in Niagara Falls, Ontario. Poorhouses were typically awful places to be, and when Scott had recovered enough to start walking again, he got out of there as soon as possible. His stroke left him in a bad condition. He had to use a cane to walk, and sometimes his legs would lock up on him and start to go numb. He knew finding work in his condition and at his age would be difficult, but Scott Mausell wasn't born with a heart of gold, and he quickly found another method to bring in an income and started his life as a con man.

Scott discovered that he could get the names and addresses of older women who were seeking husbands in their later years through matrimony bureaus. Many of them were widows and didn't want to spend their later years alone or needed the monetary support of a spouse. Scott would pick out a woman and, under a fake name, write to her. Names he commonly used were James Curtis, John Alerton, John Allen, John Williams and William Alerton. If the woman wrote back, he would send a photo of himself looking dapper or a fake photo of someone much more handsome than he was. He would always ask the woman to send his photo back to him and to tear up his letters after she read them so no one would know they were corresponding and to keep things private. If Scott thought he got a woman to take his bait, he would ask her to sell all of her property, collect the money and meet up with him. An example of what he wrote was found in a letter he sent to Hannah C. Thomas from Goodland, Indiana. The actual letter read:

> *I am in Grand Rapids now and will be going home inside of twenty days if nothing happens. Now if you think that one house on eighty acres will be enough for you, sell your 100, put what you don't use for furniture in the bank here. You can get seven percent free of all taxes. I have had the house and the eighty acres all built over and the barn so that it is all in good shape. Please send my photo when you write. Get ready and go with me. Direct to James Allen, 306 Ionia Ave, Grand Rapids, care of Fred Hilton. I will let the man that is now in the old house run the dairy as it is hard work for you and me. We will raise poultry and strawberries.*

Scott was writing hundreds of letters to women all over the United States in the hopes that one of them would do as he asked them to. If one did, his plan would be to meet her, take her money and disappear. The police never figured anything out because of his many fake identities. He thought it was brilliant.

Scott Mausell's photo he would send to women he was looking to lure in. *From* Grand Rapids Herald.

A SHADY PAST

Scott was originally from the tiny village of Mancelona in northwest Michigan. He owned farmland there, just a couple miles south of the village, as early as 1880. As a farmer, Mausell was a success, but the people of Mancelona didn't have pleasant memories of him and remembered Scott as a hot-tempered and unfriendly man. The police had been out to his property on more than one occasion, and sometimes guns were drawn on both sides. The *Grand Rapids Press* reported that his "family and neighbors always lived in fear of his fiery anger and disregard for the law." It was even rumored that he had killed his two sons.

When Scott's oldest son, Alvah, was thirty-six years old, he lived with his parents on their farm in Mancelona and worked as a log sawyer. On November 12, 1904, his logging partner said Alvah hadn't worked that afternoon and no one had seen him for some time. A search the next day found his body not far from their farmhouse. Half of his head was blown off from a shotgun blast. The death was ruled suspicious by the police and locals in Mancelona, and a coroner's inquest was called. It was said Scott and his son had been in a heated argument that Saturday and no one would put it past his awful temper to actually fire a gun at his own son. The coroner's jury came to the conclusion that Alvah had shot himself accidentally while hunting alone.

In 1910, Scott and his wife went down to Missouri to live with his younger son Elmer and his wife and children. After a few months of Scott living with them, Elmer died at the age of thirty-four. When people back home in Michigan heard Scott's son had died, it seemed suspicious to them that it had happened to Elmer when his father had come to live with him, but his death was not ruled suspicious, and his death certificate states he died of "ulcerative laryngitis."

At the end of December 1905, Scott went to spend the New Year's holiday with his older sisters, Debby and Eliza, in Pennsylvania. His sisters were considered a couple of old spinsters in their eighties and lived in the old family home everyone had grown up in. On New Year's Eve, Scott left the sisters' house to go visit a friend. When he came back later that night, he found his sister Eliza on the kitchen floor. A Winchester rifle was on top of her, and the top of her head was blown off. Debby was found outside in a woodshed, also shot to death. It was another suspicious death, and Scott was at the center of it, but the coroner's inquest ruled it as a murder and suicide. The county detective felt that Eliza first chased her sister outside and killed her in the shed and then turned the rifle on herself by using a stick to push the trigger down while she lay on the floor. Scott was a free man and not convicted of killing his sisters. He most likely came back to Michigan with some money from their estate.

THE MYSTERY WOMAN IN THE WOODS

Scott finally was excited when one of the women he had been writing for six weeks agreed to come meet him in person. Her name was Hannah St. John, and she would be traveling by train from New York to Grand Rapids on September 19, 1916. Hannah believed everything told her in his letters, and why shouldn't she? Why would the man be lying to her? Wasn't he just an older man looking for a wife? He told her his name was James Allen and that he owned a farm. They would do light jobs around the farm, like picking strawberries in the summer, and just enjoy their life together. He told Hannah to look for a man wearing a red bandanna with a large mustache when she arrived at the station.

As the train pulled into Grand Rapids, Hannah looked out the window at the people waiting outside and saw an older man wearing a red bandanna, sporting a bushy mustache. Hannah exited the train, walked up to Scott and introduced herself. Two hours later, they were husband and wife, married by Reverend Gerrit Kooiker at the Bethel Reformed Church. Curiously, Hannah lied on her marriage certificate and said her name was Anna Johnson and that she was fifty-eight years old; she was really sixty-eight. Hannah was actually still married to her second husband, Warren St. John, who was living in Wisconsin. They had been separated for a year, and she had been living in New York near some of her children. Her new husband stated his name was James Allen. After the marriage, they went to the Lincoln House, where Hannah's new husband had been renting a room.

The next day, Scott suggested they go for a picnic lunch in an area known as Beckwith's Woods, which was on the outskirts of the city, quiet and secluded. When they arrived, Scott found a good spot, and the two spread out a blanket and started to unpack their food from the basket. While they began to eat, the conversation turned to money. Hannah told him she had brought eighty-one dollars with her and would be getting more the following spring. Finding eighty-one dollars sufficient, Scott pulled out a revolver and pointed it at his new bride. He ordered her to hand over her money.

Shocked at the sudden turn of events, Hannah refused, and with that, Scott fired his gun and killed Hannah. He quickly rummaged through her pockets and found the money. Blood was soaking into the ground, and he tried to clean up the area a bit. He folded Hannah's hands over her chest, smoothed out her clothing, shoved her body under a bush and casually walked away like nothing had happened.

Back at the Lincoln House, he pulled out a pen and paper and wrote a letter to Hannah's family, telling them to go on and send the rest of her things to Cadillac, Michigan, where she would now be living. He felt that would help cover up the crime and trick everyone as to where she went, leaving him a free man to go about his business. After all, he had other letters from women to respond to.

Hannah's body wasn't found until Sunday, October 1, 1916, "one mile north of the Michigan Street road and a mile east of the city limits." Sixteen-year-old Erlie Stevens and thirteen-year-old Lewis Tenchinck were in the woods playing when they discovered her body. She had been left there to rot for nine days. It was likely a gruesome sight for young boys to stumble upon and one they probably never forgot. The boys ran home and told their parents what they had found, and the police were contacted right away.

When officers inspected the body, they had no idea who the woman was. Her face was far too decomposed to gather a good facial description, but they could note she was around five feet, four inches, 155 pounds and had gray, almost white hair. They estimated her age to be in her fifties, which was younger than she actually was. Her patent-leather shoes were new, and she had on a nice dress with beautiful lace around the collar and cuffs that was torn. They found a set of fake teeth in her pocket but nothing on her person that gave away her identity.

Surveying the area, the police could tell a desperate struggle had gone on. Hannah had been shot twice in the head, and there was a gunshot wound in her right arm. Coroner LeRoy determined that she had used her right arm to block the first bullet, which had pierced her arm and lodged itself just below her right eye. The other bullet was behind her right ear and was the one that had ended her life. The police noted the way the murderer had folded her arms neatly over her chest, which they considered disturbing.

Her body description was sent over the wires, and a response came back from Elkhart, Indiana. Her size fit the description of Addie M. Kimbal, who had not been seen in a while, but the Grand Rapids police were not confident it was the same woman and kept searching for clues. The police began their investigation by asking people in the area if they had seen anything suspicious. Ludwig Galant remembered seeing an older man and woman walking off toward the woods on Michigan Street about a week prior. The man held a picnic basket and walked with a cane. Later that afternoon, Ludwig saw the same man come back from the woods but without a basket, and the woman wasn't with him.

The most important clue came when Celia Buckley contacted police and notified them about a strange bag that had been left at the store she owned. She told investigators that a man had dropped off the bag the previous week and told her someone by the name of "Smith" would pick it up, but no one ever came to claim it. Curious what was inside the bag, Celia opened it and found a gun; part of a torn, bloody coat; and some ears of corn. After hearing about the unknown murdered woman found in the woods, she wondered if the man who had left the bag with her had something to do with the murder. She gave police a description of the man who had dropped off the bag that fit "James Allen." Ludwig had described very similar features.

The police took the bag from Celia's store and went to Foster Stevens & Co. to have the gun identified. The man there told police the gun had been purchased by William Alerton of 44 Commerce Avenue. This led police to that address, where the owner turned over a yellow bag that had belonged to "William Alerton." Inside were found letters to Hannah St. John from her children, including one from her daughter urging her mother to first get a divorce before marrying another man. The police were pretty certain they had just learned the identity of the murdered woman. Mrs. Bingham, who worked at the Lincoln House hotel, recognized the nice lace that had been on Hannah's dress and was able to tell police she remembered the woman and she had been staying there with a man named James Allen. That's when the police knew they had found their murderer and went to the Harig Farm, where they knew he was working in the cornfields.

When the police arrived at the farm, those working in the cornfield around Scott watched his face "pale" as Sheriff Berry and a few other officers approached him from behind, asking him the question, "What did you do with the coat and hat of the woman you murdered?" Scott dropped the cornhusker he was working with and turned around to face his accusers. Panic spread through him, but he quickly regained his composure and calmly replied, "What coat and hat are you talking about?" To jog his memory, they arrested him and brought him back to the very spot where he had killed Hannah to see how he would react. Scott at first denied everything the police asked him and even laughed at them, saying he didn't know who the woman was and certainly hadn't been married to her. What

Scott didn't know was just how much background work the police had done before arresting him.

Scott could deny his involvement all he wanted, but six people had been able to identify him as the man the police were looking for. He was told his room and trunks had been searched at the Lincoln House hotel, and when the police searched through his things, they found a marriage certificate for a "James Allen and Anna Johnson" made out on September 19, 1916. He denied that it was his certificate, saying he was just holding onto it for someone else. The police told him how Celia Buckley and her husband, along with Ludwig Galant, had identified Scott as the man who had dropped off the bag and who had been seen walking with Hannah on Michigan Street. The evidence against him was stacking up, and his story started to waver just a little. He admitted that he had married her after police told him the license clerk, who was a witness on the certificate, had also identified Hannah and him.

He said that she abandoned him two days after they were married and took off to Cadillac with friends to look at some property she had an interest in buying. He figured maybe this lie would work, seeing as to how he had written her family about her living in Cadillac. The police continued with their "severe sweating," as they called it back then, and asked question after question, knowing full well the man was guilty and a confession would come sooner or later.

He finally admitted he had shot her but thought he would try one more lie before totally confessing. Scott tried the self-defense angle and said that it was *Hannah* who had tried to attack and rob him, and seeing he was old and frail, he had to protect himself, so he shot her. He admitted that after the attack, he just went back to work, not knowing what else to do, as he didn't want to get in trouble. Police didn't buy that story either, and while being detained at the police station, Scott finally gave up and admitted he had killed Hannah for her money.

The story spread quickly and appeared in newspapers all over the nation. Reporters didn't even know which name to use at first and just picked one of his many aliases to tell the story of the "Michigan mail-order murder," as a Nebraska paper coined it. The *Denver Post* compared him to a male version of the infamous Belle Gunness, a Norwegian-born female serial killer who had moved to the United States. She made it her life's work to kill off her boyfriends and husbands to collect money from their life insurance policies, along with inheriting the money they had and any of their belongings. It was even said she had killed her own children. She was never caught, and it was said Belle may have been responsible for about forty deaths. It was certainly a good comparison because as news of Scott's crime spread, police departments in other states such as Alabama, Idaho, Iowa and Indiana started to take a double look at their cold case files and wondered if Mausell could have been responsible for some of them.

Police sent out the names of the women he had been writing to so the police in each state could get in touch with those women to make sure they were all still alive. Thankfully, they were. No other crimes could be pinned on Scott, as the evidence wasn't there. It was thought he had possibly married at least a dozen other women and taken their money, but once he confessed about killing Hannah, he shut his mouth and wouldn't tell the cops anything more about his life. He said, "I don't believe in telling all I know. It don't get you anything." The *Denver Rocky Mountain News* reported that when asked about his past unknown misdeeds, he responded, "I have got to go to prison for the rest of my life and I will talk no more. If the court had been a little easy on me, a man so old, I might have told more. They may investigate my past, they can charge me with the murder of my son, but I will never admit it. I'll admit nothing now."

Hannah's son from her first marriage, William Galati, was living in Elmira, New York, and was notified that his mother had been killed in Grand Rapids, Michigan. He came to collect her body, but not having any extra money, he had to write to other family members and sit and wait to hear back from them. Finally, plans were made to send her body to a relative in Ridgeland, Wisconsin. She was buried in Vanceburg Cemetery in Prairie Farm, Wisconsin.

Scott actually had the audacity to suggest that the money police had confiscated from a bank account and his room belonged to him and that it should not be used to help defray the funeral costs of the woman he had murdered. He was absolutely heartless and had no remorse for the crime he committed. "Let the county pay for the funeral," he barked.

On October 4, 1916, seventy-one-year-old Scott Mausell was sentenced to life in prison at Jackson for first-degree murder. It was one of the fastest sentences ever given in Kent County and only cost the county a total of thirty dollars, a record low. Scott seemed to be comfortable with his sentence. He wouldn't be going back to a poor farm, and he wouldn't have to worry about an income anymore. When reporters interviewed him after his sentencing, he stated, "I'm not sorry. It was either the jail or the poorhouse. I'm getting so I can't work anymore, and if they only give me a little tobacco at Jackson and let me get out in the open that's all I want."

Old Jackson Prison. *Courtesy of Library of Congress.*

He died in prison three years later. The money he had saved during his jail time paid for his burial in the prison cemetery. If Scott did commit other murders, including the suspicious death of his son Alvah, he took his secrets with him to the grave like he wanted, only sharing them with the devil himself.

Chapter 2

Notorious Clem Blood

O ne could argue that Clement "Clem" Blood didn't stand a chance.
Born in Indiana but raised in Kalamazoo, Clem didn't grow up in
the greatest of environments with a loving, happy family. His mother and
father didn't get along or raise their children with the best of standards.
Nearly all his brothers and sisters got into some form of trouble or made
news headlines. By the age of eight, Clem had already run away from home,
hopping on a train to Grand Rapids, but was caught by the conductor and
promptly brought back to Kalamazoo and turned over to the police.

When he turned fourteen, Clem and his friend Isaac, who was only ten,
broke into a store and stole items such as candy, tobacco and food. They
were caught and taken to jail. At age sixteen, Clem was sent to the state
reform school for one year. Deciding prison life was not his thing, he escaped
and was later found hiding back home; his mother, Sarah, concealed him in
a closet and claimed he wasn't there when police came looking.

By age nineteen, Clem still couldn't control his criminal instincts. On
January 18, 1893, he was picked up for stealing someone's coat. Three
months later, on March 28, while he was working for a William Stoddard, the
Kalamazoo Gazette reported that Clem crossed the street to a neighbor's house
and made himself at home, stealing "a Winchester rifle, a box of cartridges,
a hunting coat, shirt, razor and a bag of provisions and had eaten a cherry
pie and drank a quart of milk." He vanished early from work that day before
anyone knew things had been stolen. Not having to guess too hard who the
culprit was, police went to Clem's home to arrest him. As they made the

arrest, Clem told the police that he would have "made it interesting for the officers if he had the rifle with him." Clem didn't argue the larceny charge, and everything he stole was returned to the owner, but he was sentenced to the Ionia House of Correction for three and a half years, his longest sentence to date. Newspapers reported, "He was so incensed when given the sentence to the Ionia prison that he tore every shred of clothing from his body. He was presented a new suit at public expense."

No matter how many fits of anger or prolonged stays at the prisons, nothing seemed to steer him toward a brighter future. The man was hell-bent on a life of crime, and he seemed born to do nothing else. When Clem got out of Ionia after three and a half years, he and his younger brother Vernon were arrested on November 9, 1896, for carrying concealed weapons. They were put in jail, and the doctors had to be called in when Clem decided to take some opium he had on him to try and kill himself, claiming frustration over not being able to find good work. The doctors saved him, and when the brothers were released, they were fined twenty-three dollars or a thirty-day stay in jail. Not having any money, they chose jail time.

A couple months later, on January 8, 1897, Sheriff Snow suspected Clem and Vernon of shooting and stealing sheep after tracking footprints that led straight to the Blood household. Sheriff Snow had only been on the job for one week and hadn't yet dealt with the highly volatile Clem Blood but had no doubt been briefed on his antics. Sheriff Snow approached the Blood house with caution. He saw Vernon outside and started to question him about another crime he was working on. Wanting to get an idea where Clem was, Snow asked casually, "Where's your brother at, Vernon?"

"Oh, he just left the house," Vernon replied. Snow didn't really believe that, and before he knew it, Clem had stepped out of the house and yelled, "Get off my property or I'll fill you full!" Clem lifted and aimed a shotgun toward the sheriff and Undersheriff Eberstein. The two men knew the situation could go from bad to worse. Clem Blood wasn't a stable man and didn't have much respect for anything, let alone the law. The men started to back away from the Blood property. Snow slowly started to draw his gun in case he needed it. Clem noticed the sheriff going for the gun. That was enough to set Clem off, and he fired at the sheriff. Birdshot pelted down and stung the sheriff and embedded itself in his leg and one of his pinky fingers, breaking the bone.

Quickly assessing his injuries and determining that they were not life threatening, Sheriff Snow chased after the now twenty-one-year-old Clem after he dropped his gun and made a run for it. After a long chase, Clem, out

An antique postcard of Jackson Prison, 1908. *Courtesy of Library of Congress.*

Jackson Prison inmates outside. *Courtesy of Library of Congress.*

of breath and realizing he was caught, stopped and put his arms up in the air. Sheriff Snow arrested him and impressed the citizens of Kalamazoo with his capture while injured. Vernon was arrested as well for stealing the sheep, and the brothers were once again hauled off to jail, which was becoming just as familiar to them as home.

While Kalamazoo residents were happy their new sheriff was okay and healing from his minor wounds, many couldn't contain their joy that Clem Blood would finally be landing a long stay in prison that would keep him off the streets and away from endangering people. The *Kalamazoo Gazette* wrote, "Clem is surely booked for a term in Jackson prison that will make the world seem strange when he gets out." Clem was charged for assault with attempt to murder. Bail was set at $1,500, but no one bothered to pay. Clem sat in the local jail for four months until a jury was finally put together in March 1897. It was almost impossible to find jury members who didn't have a preconceived notion about Clem Blood. The court went through thirty-six men before finding people who hadn't paid much attention to the news for the past ten years.

Clem was found guilty of "assault with intent to do great bodily harm less than murder," which Clem wasn't satisfied with. He informed the judge that he wished he had been sentenced on "attempt to murder" because it sounded better to him. He was given ten years.

THE BLOOD FAMILY

Clem wasn't the only notorious one in his clan. Just about everyone in his immediate family at some point had his or her moment in the spotlight for better or for worse—usually for worse. His parents were Charles and Sarah, and their children, in order of age, were Clarence, Clem, Vernon, Nellie, Pearl, Cora and Claude (twins) and Maude.

Charles and Sarah didn't have a picture-perfect marriage and argued often, eventually separating but not divorcing. Charles was said to have "abandoned" his family after the separation. On Saturday, March 14, 1896, Sarah grabbed a hammer, flat iron and nails and headed upstairs. The children suddenly heard loud sounds and their mom screaming and yelling even though no one was with her. The *Kalamazoo Gazette* reported, "She swore vengeance on all humanity, then vowed that she would kill herself." As she still had four young kids at home at the time, they freaked out, ran outside and told the neighbors what was going on. Not even the neighbors dared go over to the house to find out what was going on. Police were called to let them deal with the family, but by the time they arrived, Sarah had already let herself out of the room and left the house. The police checked out the upstairs and saw the hammer and nails but noticed it looked like she had just knocked some plaster off the walls. It was later learned she never intended to kill herself. She was just venting over her husband, who never ceased to anger her. Sometimes you just have to hit something.

Clarence, the oldest son, was picked up numerous times for drunkenness in Kalamazoo and had been in trouble for stealing when the family lived in Indiana before moving to Michigan. On February 2, 1891, papers reported that he pleaded not guilty to disorderly conduct. Sarah told police that her husband, Charles, had started the fight that caused his arrest. Sadly, Sarah Blood was notified on July 14, 1893, that her son Clarence had passed away in Peru, Indiana, at the young age of twenty-three.

Vern, just two years younger than Clem, often mimicked what his older brother did, getting himself into trouble. On January 14, 1897, after Clem shot the sheriff, Vern was charged with "willfully abusing a sheep" and theft. Bail was set at $500. By February 11, he was sentenced to ninety days' hard labor in the county jail. Thirty-two days into his sentence, he escaped while walking outside with a chain gang. He was found a week and a half later and would be sentenced yet again for his escape after he was done serving his original time for the sheep.

In the fall of 1897, eighteen-year-old Nellie Blood was found dead in Grand Rapids. She had been staying at a hotel in the city under the fake name of Marie Burton. When she was found, no one knew who she was, but after letters in her room were gone through, the name Nellie Blood showed up on some of them. Charles heard the descriptions of the dead girl and went to Grand Rapids to view the body. He was saddened to recognize the face of his daughter.

Maude Blood, the youngest of the clan, was arrested when she was sixteen for "juvenile disorderliness." On January 20, 1905, the judge decided to send her to the Industrial School for Girls in Albion until she was twenty-one years old. The *Kalamazoo Telegraph* reported that she "has a notorious record, at one time attempting to commit suicide and has made herself generally troublesome to the officers." Not being able to get into the school right away, Maude had to spend a few months at the county poor farm, which was not a warm and friendly place to be.

Just a week after Maude was arrested, her older sister Cora Brooks was charged with stealing a gold watch from Effie Johnson a few months prior. Effie reported the watch missing and suspected Cora because she had been at her house. The police searched Cora's home but did not find a gold watch. What they didn't know was that she had given it to her brother Claude, who left town to go to Idaho.

When Claude came back to Kalamazoo, someone told police they had seen him with a gold watch that looked like the one Effie owned. Naturally, Claude had been picked up for vagrancy. The police searched him and found the stolen watch. Effie Johnson's initials that had been etched on the back had been scratched out. The police arrested Cora on their original suspicion, and she pleaded guilty. She was offered a twenty-five-dollar fine or time spent in jail. Claude pleaded "not guilty" in front of the judge, saying he had no idea that the watch had been stolen when his sister gave it to him.

On August 3, 1899, when Cora was fourteen, she disappeared from the foster home she was living in. People were nervous because "her family has a mania for suicide." Cora was described as having "a bright, sunny disposition and exceedingly pretty." Some worried she had been abducted by a stranger or even her own father. She was found five days later at her birth home. Her mother, Sarah, had been hiding her and refused to tell police why. Rather than being sent back to the foster home, where she obviously didn't want to be, Cora and her older sister Pearl went to Grand Rapids to live with their father, Charles, who was a shoe repairman in the city.

In 1901, Cora tried to kill herself with laudanum. She almost succeeded in her attempt, but a doctor was able to revive her. The *Kalamazoo Gazette* wrote that she had been "moody and despondent" over her sister's death. Just a month before Cora's suicide attempt, Pearl, the only family member who seemed to stay out of trouble, had died on February 21, 1901, from influenza at the age of nineteen.

Clem was always willing to stick up for a member of his family. Just a week before the incident with Sheriff Snow, one of Clem's little sisters who was still in school told her big brother that the teacher had been mean to her. Clem didn't want anyone messing with his family, especially his little sister, so he made an appearance at the school and punched the teacher in the face.

You Haven't Seen the Last of Clem Blood!

Having served eight years for shooting the sheriff, Clem was released in December 1905 and by January 12, 1906, was already making headlines with "Ex-Convict on the Warpath." The *Kalazmazoo Gazette* wrote, "Clem Blood, an ex-convict released from prison last month, had become suddenly insane and threatened to take the life of any person who interfered with him." According to reports, Clem went to the home of his brother-in-law Bert Brooks, his sister Cora's husband, and asked for the clothes Bert had been keeping for him. Bert handed them over, and Clem proceeded to shred the clothes with a razor. He left the house, armed himself with a revolver and went out to "terrorize the citizens of the east side" of Kalamazoo. The police found Clem hiding in a hut and arrested him. As the cops were taking him in, Clem screamed, "If I had my gun on me, you would all be dead!"

Was Clem acting up after having been locked up for eight long years? Was he now more comfortable being in jail than on the outside, where he had to fend for himself? Clem spent the year in and out of jail and in October 1906 was arrested for carrying concealed weapons and threatening to kill a woman whom he said owed him money. He was given thirty days in jail, but that still wouldn't be the last anyone heard from Clem Blood.

Just before Christmas 1906, Herbert Congdon, a wealthy merchant of Kalamazoo, received a threatening letter that read:

Unless you leave $100 in my room on North Rose Street sometime today, I will blow up every building you own in the city with dynamite and do it quick and I will kill you on sight. This is no idle threat and I mean every word I say. Do it, and do it quick, or my threat will be carried out to the letter. Give this letter to the police and sheriff if you want to. That will make no difference. Nothing will satisfy unless you leave the money in my room."

The author of the letter called Herbert two times on the telephone, asking him if he was going to bring the money to his room. Of course, the police suspected their favorite hometown criminal immediately but couldn't find him anywhere. According to Herbert, the last phone call he received was the man telling him to "never mind" the blackmailing, as he just happened to be drunk when he made those threats, but he wondered if he had still sent the money to his room. Herbert told the police he was confident that it had been Clem Blood on the phone.

The *Kalamazoo Gazette* wrote of Clem, "He is bright, capable and shrewd and will give the officers a good chase." Some suspected he took off to Chicago, while others felt he was just hiding in Kalamazoo somewhere. Clem might have fancied himself a professional criminal, but he always managed to get busted. The *Kalamazoo Gazette* further noted, "The officers declare that Blood is one of the worst men they have to deal with. He is a daring criminal and will fight to a finish when cornered."

Clem had last been seen at his sister Cora's house. When police showed up to search the house, Cora wouldn't let them inside and made them leave and return with a search warrant. She would help out her brother no matter what. After all, he was still family. The police came back, but Clem was nowhere to be found. In fact, he actually stayed out of the limelight for about five months. On May 1, 1909, police discovered he was working at the Michigan Central Railroad, and a heavily bearded Clem was arrested…again.

Clem denied that he had written the letter to Herbert Congdon and told police he had been living in Grand Rapids for the past two years. Two weeks later, police released Clem, as Herbert wasn't interested in pressing charges. Oddly enough, it was learned that Herbert was Clem's uncle on his mother's side. The police told Clem to leave the city and never come back, and he finally did just that, finding a new home in Grand Rapids.

DEAD MEN TELL NO TALES

On September 26, 1910, citizens of Grand Rapids were shocked by the awful murder of sixty-six-year-old grocery store owner Marinus Landman. The *Grand Rapids Press* considered the crime to be "one of the most cold blooded in the history of the city." Locking up his shop for the night, Marinus started on his walk home but would never make it that far. He was found thrown down a thirty-foot ravine, barely breathing, with the back of his skull crushed. A man approaching the area during the crime noticed two men take off running in a suspicious manner. When the man passed by the ravine, he heard moaning and saw Marinus's body.

Marinus was still alive when they found him but unconscious and not doing well. He was brought home, and someone sat by his side the entire time, hoping he would wake up and relate what had happened to him. But he never regained consciousness and passed away. Poor Marinus took his story and the identity of his attackers to the grave with him.

Investigating the area, police found a wool sock with a "rock the size of a man's fist" inside; this had been the weapon that connected with the back of Marinus's head. He had been hit so hard that his false teeth had flown out of his mouth and were found far away from his body.

Police suspected the killers could have been highwaymen, possibly the ones who had just robbed some men in Greenville a week earlier. The year before, Marinus had been attacked by some men looking to rob him on his way home, but he had been able to fight them off. The men had never been caught. Citizens in the neighborhood where Marinus was attacked were scared and asked that more lighting be installed in the area to ensure some safety, as it was too dark to begin with, which encouraged crime.

Within a couple weeks, the Grand Rapids Police Department was given a helpful tip from a factory worker. The man felt guilty about the knowledge he had and asked to speak to Detective Pete Viergever. He knew the men who had tried to rob Marinus the previous year and told their names. Viergever paid a visit to the men, who ended up confessing they had been the attackers the first time but hadn't been the culprits behind the murder. For information on that, they suggested the detective go find eighteen-year-old Arthur Shellhorn.

Shellhorn denied he had anything to do with the murder at first but finally confessed, admitting the actual mastermind behind the plot to rob Marinus was none other than the infamous Clem Blood. Arthur warned the police to be careful when they went after Clem, as the man would most likely shoot to kill if he had the chance.

The police were aware of Clem's past and knew the guy was a bit crazy. They knew it wouldn't be wise to just show up at the place he was staying on Ottawa Avenue, so they sent him a fake letter. The letter told Clem he was needed at the Clarendon Hotel, as there was a porter job available for him. Clem left the house and headed toward the hotel, where he was jumped by two officers who were able to take him down and get him to the station. In under twenty-four hours, Clem and Arthur had confessed and were charged, sentenced and on their way to prison.

Clem's face didn't show any surprise as the judge told him he would be in prison for "the rest of his natural life." Knowing that his life on the streets as a professional criminal had finally come to a close, Clem exposed a little about his past. He told the courtroom that "he was born of the wrong kind of parents" and "seemed to expect his fate." He said that "his life from infancy has been one of continuous crime and debauchery" and that "he never had a fair chance in life," having been "born from a father who was no good and a mother of the same caliber." He told of being born in Indiana and moving to Kalamazoo when he was younger. Clem admitted that he had spent fourteen and a half of his thirty-six years behind bars—nearly half of his life.

Details of the crime came out during the examination, and Clem didn't seem to have one resentful bone in his body as he told what happened the night they killed Marinus. Marinus had recognized Clem's face, so it was either kill the aged grocer or risk being caught if the man lived. Clem said, "Dead men tell no tales," so he chose to end it for Marinus, claiming that murder hadn't been the original intent.

Referred to as Blood's "understudy," eighteen-year-old Arthur Shellhorn had met him a couple weeks before the murder. Clem had been teaching a kind of "school for criminals" with some young men who lived near him. Clem glorified the criminal lifestyle, telling them how liberating it was to ignore the law and just do what you wanted. A reporter for the *Grand Rapids Press* even noted that Shellhorn seemed to have "admiration" for Clem.

Clem had got the itch to rob someone and asked his "students" if anyone knew a good victim and if anyone wanted to join in on the job to learn a thing or two. "I always work with someone," said Clem. "When the spell to do a job comes over me, it is like a disease and I cannot restrain myself." Arthur told Clem about Marinus, who had come to his attention because he remembered him being mugged once before. *Why not a second time?* he thought, as the man usually had money on him from his grocery store, so Arthur and Clem lurked in the shadows and followed Marinus for a couple

A 1909 postcard from Marquette Prison. *Author's collection.*

nights before making their move. When they jumped him on September 26, 1910, Arthur was the first to bash his head, and Clem pushed him down the ravine and continued to hit his head with the rock weapon. Twenty-seven dollars was all Marinus had on him. The two criminals split the money.

The *Kalamazoo Gazette* was happy to report that its hometown terrorizer, Clem Blood, had finally earned himself a life sentence at Marquette Prison. The paper commented that men like Clem should have been locked up to start with and never let out and allowed the chance to murder someone. The man was a career criminal and knew nothing else. Prosecutor Brown asked Clem if he had ever murdered anyone before, which made Blood smile. "I don't care to say anything about that," was all he replied.

On September 29, 1910, Arthur Shellhorn was given a life sentence. He had originally been scheduled to be in court that day for vandalizing a playground a month earlier. Instead, he was being sentenced for murder; the judge dropped the vandalism charge. Arthur's parents were divorced and had each remarried. His father had moved to Wisconsin, but none of his family in Grand Rapids was there to see him off leaving for Marquette Prison. After having been in prison for two years, Warden Russell said of him, "That boy is not a bad one at heart." Because of his good behavior, in 1916, the governor decreased Shellhorn's sentence to just ten years and not life.

A local phrenologist—someone who claims to glean personality traits through the characteristics and shape of the head—wrote an article in the *Grand Rapids Press* saying Arthur's head suggested he was "lacking in self-esteem and somewhat in self-reliance," but "had he cultivated his intellectual faculties and directed his energies along some legitimate line, he could have achieved notable and honorable success for he had ample courage, continuity and intelligence to carry out such a purpose." Clem's head, on the other hand, suggested to the phrenologist that he had a penchant for crime and was an "unusual type of criminal."

LeRoy "Red" Larson and Frank Matuszak, the men who had attempted to rob Marinus Landman on December 18, 1909, were brought into court on September 30 and charged for the crime they almost got away with.

If Clem liked to impress people with his "tough" image, he was able to boast in 1954 that if Tom Duley was released from prison for murder after having served forty-seven years, Clem would take the record for serving the longest prison record in the state of Michigan at that time, at forty-four years behind bars and counting.

Chapter 3

The Thomson Jewelry Store Robbery and Triple Murder

"This is not local talent" was the sentiment offered by police when the J.J. Thomson Jewelry store in Campau Square on Monroe Street was robbed for diamonds, leaving two men dead and one fatally injured on September 18, 1913. People on the streets heard loud pops and thought maybe a car had backfired. No one thought the sounds had been gunfire. The bandits had already dashed out of the jewelry store and disappeared before anyone knew what had even happened. From 1911 to 1913, the city seemed to suffer from an unusual amount of crime that was leaving residents shaken and scared to go about their daily business. The world was becoming a bigger place, and stories like this were becoming all too common in the national news.

It was late on a Thursday afternoon when the holdup and shooting happened. The three men working inside were startled when two men entered the store, pulled out guns and yelled, "Hold up your hands!" The men forced the store workers into a backroom, but the workers weren't going to just sit still and let the store be robbed without doing anything to try to prevent it. They fought back, but the gunmen had no guilt about using their revolvers and fired on the employees.

When the police responded to the scene, people were already gathered around the building trying to see inside. Paul Townsend was the only store clerk who was left barely alive. He had been shot in the throat, and his chance of survival wasn't good. He had only been working at the store for three months and was soon to be married. The other store workers were

J.J. Thomson Jewelry Store. *Courtesy of the Grand Rapids Public Library.*

dead when the police arrived. John Thomson, the store owner's nephew, had been shot in the heart, and George Smith's lungs had been pierced and his spinal cord severed from the gunshot.

A $2,500 reward was offered for any information that would lead police to the robbers. With reward money that high, detectives from all over rolled up their sleeves to try their hands at solving the case, but it was looking like a hopeless start, as clues were sparse and there hadn't been many good witnesses. The only excellent witness who could comment was Paul Townsend, who was able to give a statement at first to the prosecuting attorney but other than that wasn't able to speak well and was fighting for his life at Butterworth Hospital. After infection set in, he died a week later on September 22, 1913. The police were gathering up every shady character they could find and questioning them in hopes of discovering some clue that would point them in the right direction.

Store owner J.J. Thomson had been away the day his store was held up or else he would have been among the dead. Upon taking inventory, he noted the bandits had made off with thirty-five diamond rings, a watch, a couple pairs of earrings and his nephew's Tiffany ring that one of the gunmen actually took off his finger after killing him. The total value of the stolen items was about $2,200, or about $50,000 today.

The *Grand Rapids Herald* bashed the Grand Rapids police force for its work on the case in the beginning. In an article published on September 20, 1913, the paper wrote, "The city detectives are efficient in trailing small boys who break back windows and steal candy, but when it comes to coping with professional crooks who move with certainty and skill they seem as helpless as children." The reporter suggested that Grand Rapids was getting the reputation of being "an easy town to work."

THE FIRST ARREST

On October 23, 1913, Chicago man Ray Blackburn and his wife were arrested by Grand Rapids detective Peter Viergever and Chicago police. Ray was the suspect, but both he and his wife were questioned. From that conversation, two other men were arrested, James Mills and George Franklin, but confidence was low that these were the men who did the job. All the evidence the police had was circumstantial.

Ray had been picked out of a police lineup by witnesses in Grand Rapids, and a woman who went by the name of Lousy Lou told police that she knew Ray Blackburn. She said he dealt in diamonds and had been in town the day before the holdup. She had seen him and was certain that he had something to do with the robbery. Elizabeth Vanderleest also picked Ray out, saying she was confident he had something to do with the case. She said she had a party the night before the robbery and Ray, along with James and George, had been there. Not having much to work with, the police figured if a couple people had pointed Ray out, it was better than nothing.

It took a few weeks for police to legally get Ray Blackburn to Grand Rapids and out of Chicago. During the habeas corpus proceedings in Chicago in an effort to put him on trial in Michigan, over ten people said they had seen Ray around town and working at Sullivan's Saloon in Chicago the day of the Thomson robbery, but Grand Rapids got its way, and Ray was sent on to Michigan, where he demanded an examination.

A daring *Grand Rapids Press* reporter, Ed Nowak, heard the police were going to Chicago to pick up a possible suspect. He followed the men to Cook

Patrolmen of Grand Rapids in 1907. Peter Viergever is on the top right at the end. *Courtesy of the Grand Rapids Public Library.*

County, Illinois, and when Ray Blackburn was put in a car to be brought back to Grand Rapids, Ed secretly jumped on the back of the car and clung to the spare tire and was able to listen to the conversation inside the car. Ed managed to hang onto the back all the way to Gary, Indiana, but as it was November, he was freezing and couldn't hang on any longer. He hopped off and got a train ticket back to Grand Rapids—but not before calling back home and letting out the exciting story that one of the possible killers from the Thomson case had been discovered and was being brought back to Grand Rapids.

Ray's trial began with a packed courtroom on November 13, 1913, and immediately was in his favor. Elizabeth Vanderleest, who was so positive Ray was their man, said "she cannot identify Blackburn as the man who rented a room of her," admitting that Ray was much younger looking than the man she had earlier claimed to recognize. Everyone was saying that Ray had an "amazing likeness" to the person they saw on September 18, but the person they saw wasn't Ray Blackburn. Ernest Rose said he had been by the door of the jewelry store when the men ran out with Paul Townsend feebly trying to chase after them. Ernest said one man was much shorter than the other, and he was certain Ray had been one of them.

The preliminary hearing was bound over to the superior court. Ray's attorney, Edward Barnard, considered one of Chicago's greatest criminal lawyers, tried to get the case dismissed on "grounds of insufficient testimony," but the judge ruled against it.

Meanwhile, the police were still busy arresting other men, such as Jerry Thomas and James Kendall, who were hardened criminals. Kendall had a tough face and was considered an expert on burglary. Thomas looked the part of a criminal back then. The *Grand Rapids Press* reported on his completely tattooed body and listed what the images were: a Chinese dragon, a mermaid, American flags, a woman and cross, a rose, a heart, a snake, an anchor, a woman's head, an eagle, a butterfly, a Confederate flag and the potentially regrettable women's names Nellie, Rose and Ethel on different parts. Neither man was held long, and they were let go after questioning.

When the case resumed, it dragged on and at one point was likened to a vaudeville show. The lawyers went back and forth with each other and often sent laughter through the crowded courtroom. By March 28, 1914, there wasn't enough evidence to convict Ray of being involved in the crime, and he was granted his freedom. The police were back to the drawing board again for suspects.

Not giving up on the case, the dedicated and brilliant Detective John Halloran got a clue from a man who told him to head to Detroit, which then sent him onward to Toledo, where he spent a couple weeks in disguise to get in good with the underworld. Toledo was known to be a sanctuary for criminals at the time. Much to Halloran's surprise, a few of Thomson's missing diamonds showed up in a Toledo pawnshop. Halloran was excited and knew he was finally onto something. Grand Rapids had already spent a lot of money on the trial of Ray Blackburn, but Sheriff O'Donnell of Grand Rapids believed Halloran was on the right path and gave him $300 of his own money to continue his undercover work in Ohio.

Halloran started to talk to anyone he could in order to get names. Acting as a cigar salesman, he got to know a businessman who started to tell him about two men who had tried to sell him some loose diamonds. The businessman described a "tall, dark haired fellow" who was with a man named "Chippy" Robinson and a woman. Halloran located the woman and, through her, learned that the unknown man was named Walter "Vopper" Lawrence, who had come to Toledo just two days after the Thomson store holdup. Pawn store owners remembered Vopper because he had two missing fingers on his right hand.

Grand Rapids detectives. Second row and third from the left is Detective John Halloran. *Courtesy of the Grand Rapids Public Library.*

Chippy's and Vopper's descriptions were sent through the wire around the United States. The first to be picked up was Vopper in Covington, Kentucky, after he was arrested for disorderly conduct; a baker had accused him of trying to rob his store. When confronted about the Thomson Jewelry Store in Grand Rapids, Vopper said he knew nothing about it and hadn't been in the city on that day. Ironically, Vopper's father had been a policeman for twenty-five years, and his parents were well-respected citizens in Covington, but their son had a police record a mile long, mostly for robbing places. His mother was beside herself, and even though her son had robbed places before, she felt he wasn't guilty and said she "would spend her last cent to save her son." When she hugged him goodbye before the police took him away, she tucked a sandwich into his pocket and told him she loved him.

As Vopper had escaped police once before, Detective Halloran wasn't taking any chances with him. He had been working too hard and too long on the case to have the man escape. So he chained himself to Vopper while on their way to Grand Rapids from Kentucky. A crowd waited at the train station in the hopes of catching a glimpse of the criminal, but the onlookers were disappointed when he didn't arrive until late in the evening and was quickly taken to police headquarters. Vopper felt like he was being set up because of his past misdeeds that would no doubt make him "appear" guilty to any jury.

Vopper arrived in Grand Rapids on April 17. His examination was scheduled for April 28, and he was held without bail. He was tossed in a cell that was normally reserved for drunk and disorderly women that was without a bed. No one at the jail was allowed to talk to him.

Before a warrant was even sent out for Chippy Robinson, Vopper was told that Chippy had admitted Vopper had killed the men in the jewelry store. This got Vopper so mad that he decided to tell all, saying that Chippy was the mastermind behind the whole thing and the one who had done all the shooting. In a written confession, Vopper told how he met Chippy and how they started to travel together, going to fairs where they could easily pickpocket and rob people, but Chippy wanted to go bigger. Vopper had no idea just how dangerous Chippy was. He wanted to move on to robbing banks and jewelry stores. He had suggested this to his last partner in crime, who wisely left him, not wanting to get that deeply involved. Chippy urged Vopper to "think big," and the two had many arguments over the topic. Vopper wasn't interested in the big time either.

In his confession written on June 18, he said Chippy had discovered the "artificial courage" that came to him when he was given a few drinks, so Chippy used that to his advantage. Filling Vopper with "liquid courage," he got him to get up enough nerve to commit his first jewelry store robbery. "I will say I have a good heart but a bad head and that's the cause of all my trouble," Vopper wrote. Sentence was delayed, though, in the hopes that Chippy, once caught, would confess and add to the story.

A warrant for the arrest of Lawrence "Chippy" Robinson was finally announced on June 16, 1914, along with a $2,000 reward. A picture of Chippy was discovered in the Cincinnati "rogues' gallery" and sent around to police agencies all over the country. A few days later, on June 19, police in Boston were told that someone by the name of "Chippy" Robinson was in town and someone had spotted him eating at the Boylston Café. Detective Thomas Norton of the Boston police and a few other officers decided to go to the restaurant and make the arrest.

It was the afternoon, and the café was busy with people. Musicians played music that blended with the conversations of the diners. Detective Norton and four officers entered the cafe dressed in street clothes and spotted their man. Norton approached Chippy from the front, announcing to him, "I arrest you for the murder of three men in Grand Rapids, Michigan." Chippy looked shocked but got up out of his seat as if he were going to allow the men to arrest him. Before anyone could react, Chippy moved fast. He pulled a gun from his suit jacket and shot Detective Norton at close range in the stomach. Everything happened so fast that even the piano player continued her ragtime melody without stopping until she realized a commotion was brewing.

When it was realized what had happened, the restaurant became bedlam, and the other police officers started to open fire on Chippy after Detective Norton dropped to the ground. Diners who had been out for a casual meal found themselves in the center of a crime novel. People screamed and ran for the door. Chippy took off running, even though he had been shot three times. He was able to get out of the building by hiding in the panicked crowd fleeing the restaurant. Once outside, he didn't get far and collapsed just around the building in an alleyway. A mounted policeman saw him fall to the ground and rode up to him. As the police grabbed Chippy and dragged him off the ground, the click of his empty gun could still be heard as he tried to fire it. He had no idea that the clip had fallen out of his gun in the restaurant. According to an article on the *Kent County Michigan GenWeb Project*, "The case had its effect on the Colt Arms Company. The designers corrected the faulty positioning of the magazine lock so nobody would again find himself in 'Chippy's' position of trying to fire an empty gun." When Chippy was brought into custody, he denied having any involvement with the Grand Rapids murders.

Over one thousand people gathered outside the courthouse to witness the well-dressed, six-foot, three-inch criminal being escorted inside. The courtroom usually held two hundred, but six hundred people had pushed their way inside to watch the start of the proceedings. Chippy pleaded not guilty to killing Detective Norton, claiming self-defense. While he stood in front of the judge, he had a cool and calm demeanor, even smiling at times. After a search of his things at a Boston hotel, the police discovered many expensive and fine clothes. They were shocked to learn that Chippy was quite the smooth criminal. Reports from Boston said he was leading a "double life as a traveling salesman and a promoter" and had access "to some of the best homes of Boston." He hid behind the guise of a man with good taste, and it was even said he had taken dance lessons so he could mingle with the finest in society. The Boston police figured the Thomson store robbery was his steppingstone to bigger heists that quickly turned him into a "gentleman crook" rather than the shabby two-bit one he had been in the past. The Boston newspapers referred to him as "Diamond Club Robinson." Police discovered a deposit box that held "a fortune in diamonds and cash" that

Chippy Robinson on trial in Boston. *From* Grand Rapids Herald.

only he had access to. He even had hidden pockets sewn into his suits that he would use to hide diamonds in.

His trial was set for July 20, 1914. On July 22, Chippy was escorted back to jail after the court session was closed for the day, but that would be the last day of the trial. Alone in his cell, Chippy disassembled his shoe, removed a piece of steel from it and sharpened it into a shank. He wrapped a blanket around himself to absorb the blood so it wouldn't flow from his body and under the cell door, alerting police to his suicide attempt and potentially saving him. By the time someone in the jail checked on him, Chippy was dead. He had used the shank to slash his throat and a wrist. The news was kept quiet, and when everyone gathered back into the courtroom on the third day, it was announced that Chippy had killed himself—the trial was over.

Letters were found in his cell. One note admitted he was sorry for how he had treated his wife. They had been married for fourteen years, and when he was arrested, he hadn't been by her side much and she was dying of tuberculosis. With his newfound life of high crime and instant money, he had plenty of other women he kept on the side. The other letter began with, "It's a tough game when you have to die to beat it."

For being an accomplice in the crime, Vopper was sentenced to seven to fifteen years at Marquette Prison on July 28, 1914. Because he confessed, he was given the lesser sentence of manslaughter versus first-degree murder. He made extra money on the train to prison by selling his autograph to fellow train riders.

All the stolen diamonds had been expertly recovered during the nearly yearlong search to find the men who had held up the J.J. Thomson Jewelry store and were responsible for three deaths. The criminals might have never been found if it hadn't been for the efforts of Detective John Halloran and his amazing tenacity and detective skills.

Chapter 4

The Jealousy of Frank Loeffler

Frank Loeffler wasn't doing so well. His mind as of late was chaotic with thoughts of beautiful twenty-two-year-old Louisa Yakel, the love of his life. Somehow, he had convinced himself she was going to become a nun in a convent and he would never be able to marry her. She would be locked up in a church somewhere devoted only to God. Frank couldn't bear the thought of it. Ideas started to race through his mind about how to prevent it from happening. Things became foggy and scattered inside his mind. He knew what he had to do to end his suffering.

On Monday, July 4, 1904, everyone in Grand Rapids was celebrating the country's independence, relaxing, enjoying time with family and setting off fireworks. No one expected Grand Rapids to be rocked with tragedy that day, but Frank Loeffler would see to it that it was.

Born in the Czech Republic in 1865, Frank immigrated to the United States in 1882 and found work in Alpine Township on Jacob Yakel's farm. He was a petite man with small blue eyes and was a good worker. He became a familiar face and a family friend around the Yakel household. The year Frank began working on the farm, Jacob's wife, Elizabeth, had just welcomed her third daughter, Louisa, into the world.

After a number of years, Frank left the farm to work for the Manistee Lumber Company in northern Michigan, where he lost a leg in an accident. The effects of the injury left him struggling physically and mentally, and by 1904, he was considered an "elderly cripple" at age thirty-nine. He ended up moving to Deighton, Michigan, and still kept in touch with the Yakel

Pretty Louisa Yakel. *From* Grand Rapids Herald.

family, stopping by their house when he was in Grand Rapids. He especially enjoyed visiting when Louisa was around and, before he moved, Frank asked her if they could write to each other. Louisa was now a young woman who had grown up around Frank. She felt sorry for him and told him it would be okay if he wrote to her occasionally.

Frank wrote often, and each time, Louisa would politely write him back. Eventually, Louisa started to feel uncomfortable around him, as he had developed the annoying habit of proposing to her. At first, she just laughed it off and, in keeping with her nice demeanor, told him she wasn't interested. But the proposals didn't stop. He was twice her age, and she simply didn't think of Frank as a potential husband. After he had stopped by the house one day in Grand Rapids, he made Louisa feel bad by releasing a long sigh and saying, "A cripple like me will never find happiness." Feeling sorry for the man, she sat with him a while and talked, probably giving him words of encouragement that he would find someone out there. But Frank didn't want just "someone"; he wanted Louisa.

Even though Louisa asked him to stop his proposals, he didn't quite get the message. In one of her letters she had written back to Frank that he kept, she said, "Talk of dreaming…you certainly are or are you demented? My God. Is my cup of sorrow not full to overflowing? Must I be persecuted beyond endurance? I see you will not use common sense." She asked him to stop writing to her, to stop the proposals and to "release her of her promise" to write him occasionally. It was clear by these few lines that Louisa had had enough of his affections and wanted him to stop. She wanted it clear to him that she would not marry him. But for Frank, their correspondence meant something. The sheer fact that she had written to him meant there must be some feelings toward him.

West Bridge Street between 1900 and 1910. *Courtesy of Library of Congress.*

Beautiful Jefferson Street, circa 1905–20. *Courtesy of Library of Congress.*

Frank decided to come to Grand Rapids for the Fourth of July and got a room at the Western Hotel on Bridge Street near Brown's Shoe Store, where Louisa was a clerk. Frank wanted to see Louisa so he could apologize for upsetting her in his letters. Louisa lived at home with her elderly mother, Elizabeth, on Jefferson Street and a couple who rented a few rooms from them in the back of the house to help with bills. When he got into town, Frank went to their home, where he later said the family was "cool" toward him. Louisa didn't have time to talk; she had plans to go out with her friends and needed to get ready. Anger and jealousy passed over his face. Elizabeth noticed him clench his fists.

He had been in the habit of stopping by more and more in the past few months when he was in Grand Rapids. Louisa's mother knew the man gave her daughter a bad feeling, as he seemed to be growing eerily possessive of her.

JEALOUSY IS A TERRIBLE THING

Frank needed to talk to Father Schrembs, the priest at St. Mary's Catholic Church and a good friend of the Yakel family. In Frank's mind, it was because of the priest that Louisa had plans to go into a convent. Stopping by the church, he asked the priest if they could talk. Both men took a seat, and Frank started to express his feelings for Louisa to the priest and how those feelings were not reciprocated. Frank told him it was "his fault" that she was going to move away and live in a convent.

Father Schrembs was taken aback but stayed calm and soothing. He could tell the man was upset, maybe even a little unbalanced. He told Frank that Louisa's life was hers to live and no one could force her to marry anyone she wasn't interested in, and whether she had plans to become a nun was not of his doing. He wasn't even aware Louisa had made such plans. In a kind, priestly manner, Father Schrembs told Frank to move on and let Louisa be. Frank didn't like this response and didn't get the reaction he had hoped for from the priest. He said to him, "Father, jealousy is a terrible thing. If one yields to it, it may lead to awful results." He really seemed convinced that he and Louisa were a match made in heaven and the priest should have recognized this.

What Father Schrembs didn't know was that Frank had an unloaded gun in his pocket. Frank thought that if he had loaded it beforehand, he maybe would have shot the priest. He left the church more bothered and irritated than he had been previously. His next stop was the Yakel family home but before that, he stopped to purchase ammunition.

Louisa and her mother had just finished eating lunch when someone knocked on their front door. Louisa answered the door, and her stomach lurched. It was Frank. She wasn't surprised to see him, as he had been in town the past few days and had already paid the family a visit. At first, she didn't want to let the man in, but he asked if they had a meal for him. She reluctantly let him come inside and in a nice but firm manner said that "they were not keeping a boarding house." Frank resented the comment and took a seat at the kitchen table.

Some food was brought out for him, but Frank picked at it, barely touching any of it. Louisa sat down at the table but didn't even look at Frank or talk to him much. Elizabeth went into another room. Louisa was so annoyed with the man that she just wanted him to eat and leave. Frank thought he would try just one more time and, like a scratched record, repeated, "Louisa, will you marry me?" Frustrated, she told him no, and that's when Frank jumped up from the table and put his arm around her neck. He got her into a hold she couldn't easily get out of. She struggled and pushed against him to get out of his grip. Frank held tight and, in his deranged mind, thought it would be the perfect time to propose again—by gunpoint. She would have to say yes! She wouldn't have a choice in the matter. But before he even said another word, the sounds of gunshots rang out, and Louisa felt searing pain in her arm. Frank had shot her, sending two bullets into her arm. Jealousy over Louisa had driven Frank mad.

Frank let her go, and Louisa dropped to the floor, wracked with pain. She screamed for her mother. With regret and panic sinking in fast, Frank started to run for the front door. Louisa stood up and stumbled toward him. Later claiming he didn't like seeing her suffer, Frank lifted his gun at Louisa and pulled the trigger. This time, the bullet pierced her chest, and she dropped to the ground, silent and unmoving. Frank looked at her for a moment and quickly fled the house.

Louisa's mother heard her daughter yell, and by the time she got into the kitchen to see what was going on, she found her beautiful daughter on the ground bleeding. It had only been a little over half a year since Elizabeth had found her seventy-four-year-old husband accidentally drowned in the cold winter water of the West Side Power Canal on December 18, 1903. She could barely take the heartache life had thrown at her. She screamed and called for help. The couple boarding in the back of the home came at the sound of her panicked cries, and people outside in the neighborhood heard the screams and cries for help. Louisa was carefully lifted from the floor and placed on a couch.

Meanwhile, it was said Frank was casually walking away from the house, his limp making him a noticeable figure around town. The doctor had been called for immediately, and looking ahead, Frank saw him tightly gripping his medical bag and running toward the Yakel home. The *Grand Rapids Press* claimed Frank stopped the doctor and told him exactly where to go and then, in a matter-of-fact tone, added, "I shot her."

When the doctor arrived at the house, there was nothing he could do to revive her. The bullet to the chest had severed a major artery. As the locals gathered around the home and started to piece together what had happened, an angry mob formed and went in search of Frank, as he couldn't have gone too far. No one had paid much attention when the bullets were fired because fireworks had been going off all day long.

Frank tried to get into the apartment of someone he knew, but it was locked, and he had to venture back out into the main street, where he saw Alderman Joseph Hermann. Alderman Hermann noticed the angry mob that was coming toward them, demanding Frank's life. The police hadn't shown up yet, but Alderman Hermann did his best to stand between Frank and the mob until the police arrived. He couldn't prevent a cast-iron cane coming at full speed from the crowd and whacking Frank so hard on his head that he dropped to the ground, unconscious. The police finally arrived, dumped Frank's body into the patrol wagon and got him down to the jail before the crowd got any worse. If they had had their way, they would have strung Frank up in a tree or beat him to death for the senseless act he had just committed.

When Frank came around, he found himself in a jail cell. Regret hit him hard that night, and he kept wailing out, "She was the best girl in the world. I loved her better than life and now I've killed her. I was crazy!" Frank never denied that he had been the one who killed her but he hired Attorneys Parks and Turner to defend him. The two lawyers knew that their only line of defense would be an insanity plea and that Frank's "feeble condition" had deteriorated his mind over the years.

Frank sat confined in the jail for a few days until July 7, when he had to be transferred to city hall for the coroner's inquest. As the police wagon trotted through town, angry Grand Rapids citizens followed, yelling curses and threats. The police had to shove people away just to get Frank out of the wagon and into city hall. They thought they would be smart and bring Frank back to the jail by sneaking him out a back way, but there was no tricking

The Reformatory in Ionia. *Courtesy of Tobin Buhk.*

the mob, and they continued to follow the wagon all the way back to the jail. One lady continually cursed Frank, hoping that "the vengeance of God should be visited upon him for striking down such a pure and innocent girl!" Frank was terrified and relieved to be back behind bars, where he actually felt safe.

Next, three doctors were sent for to inspect Frank's mental well-being and to confirm if they thought he was insane. It only took forty-five minutes for them to determine that Frank wasn't insane; therefore, the insanity plea would not work for Frank during the trial. When the doctors told the lawyers their client was not crazy, Turner and Parks urged Frank to plead guilty and possibly hope for a lighter sentence. Frank did this but the courts didn't go any lighter on him. By July 9, 1904, Frank was sentenced to Marquette Prison for life. During his sentencing, Frank grumbled that it was all Father Schrembs's fault and not his that Louisa had been killed.

Not wanting to be locked up in prison for life, Frank imagined a plan where he saw himself breaking free from the officers, who would then be forced to shoot him, killing him and saving Frank the effort of doing it himself. But Frank never had the stomach to actually do it. The police knew Frank was unbalanced and upset after the sentencing, and he was kept under watch twenty-four hours a day to prevent a suicide attempt.

The murder, funeral and sentencing all happened quickly. The papers were alight with gossip, and the town was talking. Was it actually Louisa's fault? Had she snubbed Frank? Had she ever had an affair with the man that caused him to become so infatuated with her? Having heard enough from the gossipy citizens, the Yakel family wrote a letter and published it in the *Grand Rapids Press* at the end of July 1904, extinguishing all the rumors that were flying about. They plainly stated that Louisa had never shown any romantic intentions toward him, had no convictions of going into a convent and had known Frank her whole life and always just wanted to be kind to him until he started to pester her with unwanted affection and proposals that were not necessary, especially after being asked to stop.

Frank ended up being transferred to the Ionia State Hospital, which was where many criminals went who were considered insane at the time. He died there eleven years later at the age of fifty.

Chapter 5

Potato Masher Murder

There's a guy who is dead downstairs and he's been murdered," a young man informed Mrs. Scott and her husband, the landlords of the apartment building the man lived in. Mrs. Scott just shook her head and said, "He's probably just been drinking," but she called the police anyway. The young man and his two friends left the building quickly and didn't wait around for the police to show up.

When the police arrived to check things out on December 16, 1921, they were greeted by a ghastly sight. Fifty-one-year-old James Minnema's small apartment on Ottawa Avenue was a total disaster. Empty and spilled liquor bottles were scattered about the floor. Clothes were strewn about. A coat stained with blood was draped over the bed. The washbasin was tinted pink with blood. When the police saw the body of James, it almost didn't look as if he were dead at first. The man was perched over his bed in "prayer position," stiffened with death. He was only half clothed and in his underwear, as if he had been trying to get undressed and ready for bed when he passed away. James's body was gathered up by the police to be examined by the coroner.

During the autopsy, a six-inch fracture from his left cheekbone to the top of his head was discovered. The coroner declared that a "slow hemorrhage" in James's brain had killed him. Outside James's apartment, police found a bloody potato masher, and it was suspected that whoever had attacked James used the masher as a weapon. The headlines used the cooking utensil to create sensational headlines, calling the crime the "masher murder."

Anyone who knew James was contacted to find out why this rather unsuspecting man had been brutally attacked and killed. Leonard Minnema, James's older brother, told reporters and police he had been divorced from his second wife for five years and had gained a stepson, Alfred Riddle, who still kept in contact with James. Police made sure to question him closely, and Alfred was able to tell police that his former stepdad was making moonshine. He had stopped by to visit with him a week prior to his murder, and James was complaining of not feeling well, saying that "the moonshine was getting to him."

James Minnema. *From* Grand Rapids Herald.

Mrs. Scott, the landlady, said she had never had any problems with James, but in the past few months, he had started to drink heavily. She knew he was making his own home-brew in his room. He had told her it was only for "personal use," but Mrs. Scott suspected he was selling it on the side. Prohibition in the United States had been in effect for almost two years at this point. Mrs. Scott also said she had heard James arguing loudly with someone about a week before the murder. Was it possible that James was getting in over his head with bootlegging and starting to make some enemies in the underworld of Grand Rapids?

An insurance policy listed Ethel Monroe as a beneficiary for $3,000. There was also a picture of her in James's apartment. Police learned she was living in Kalamazoo and contacted her right away, telling her about James's death and asking if she was able to shed any light on the murky situation. Ethel was unaware that she had been on his insurance policy. Ethel Monroe and his sister, Wilhelmina Harings, were both to split anything James owned equally. Ethel was his friend, and tenants in the building remembered seeing her around occasionally and said she cooked meals for him sometimes. Ethel wasn't aware of any enemies that James had or who would want to do him any harm.

Leonard Minnema had no clue who Ethel was and was shocked that she was in his will. It was obvious that James had strong feelings for her, even if he had never let her know. Leonard had been worried about his little brother for the past few years. James had come from the Netherlands, and after spending twelve years in the Dutch navy, he decided to follow his older brother to the United States and settled down in Grand Rapids. Besides two marriages and two divorces, James led a fairly quiet life. For a couple decades, he was a truck driver for the Consumer's Ice Company but had quit working there the previous summer. Leonard hadn't seen much of his brother for about a year, and when he did happen to run into him, he told him to quit making moonshine, as it would surely lead him down the wrong path. As Frank had not been employed anywhere for a while, Leonard knew where his brother's money was coming from.

The police started to suspect that James had been attacked after a fight broke out over the moonshine he was selling, possibly over money owed. They knew he had been producing liquor, as his distilling equipment was found when the apartment was searched. Coroner LeRoy felt that someone had attempted to revive James before he died. The strange facts that his bloody coat was at the end of the bed, his pants were stuffed in a dresser drawer and James was half naked, along with blood in various locations all over the dirty room, left investigators scratching their heads. Police figured James had been fully dressed when he was attacked in the alley behind his apartment, came inside and, not knowing how bad his injury was, started going about this usual business until he collapsed on his bed, dead.

Weeks went on, and it was looking like an impossible murder to solve. Detective Garrett Doyle had been following up on a stolen watch case that involved twenty-seven-year-old Elmer Matthews. He took a trip out to Coopersville to talk to Inez Buskirk, who had a recent relationship with him after leaving her husband in Jackson. Detective Doyle started to ask her about Elmer, and that's when she told the detective that Elmer was the one who had killed James Minnema. He had told her the next day when he came to her looking for money to get himself out of the state to Warrensburg, Missouri. She said Elmer had planned to murder James for $200 he believed he had hidden in his apartment. He also got a couple friends involved in the plot: twenty-three-year-old Edward Murphy and his wife, who lived in the same apartment building as James.

John Grzeskowiak, a taxi driver, came forward and told Detective Doyle he believed he had given a man who fit Elmer's description a ride to Ottawa Avenue the night James was murdered. The man told the taxi driver to drop him off near the alleyway behind James's apartment. John noted the man had been drinking, and before he got out of the car, he said, "If I don't come back in 10 minutes, you'll know something is wrong. I'm going to get some money a man owes me." Ten minutes went by, and John didn't see any sign of the man. He continued to wait.

Thirty minutes later, the man came back, jumped into the taxi and told the driver to take him to Coopersville. John asked him if he was able to pay, and that's when the man casually pulled a razor out of his pocket, twirling it around in his hand. He told the driver his father would pay him. Not liking the situation or the silent threat the man was suggesting with his blade, John kicked him out of his car and drove away. It wasn't until the details about Elmer came out in the papers that the driver started to make a connection with the man in his cab that night and went to police headquarters. He told them what had happened in his cab the night of December 15, 1921.

The Murphys were picked up and detained by police. It was believed the wooden potato masher had come from Mrs. Murphy's kitchen. Shortly after James's body was found dead in his apartment, Mrs. Murphy told the landlady she wanted to move to an upstairs apartment because she claimed she felt the ghostly face of James staring at her from his doorway—or was that just a guilty conscience staring back at her?

Elmer had worked with the Murphys at the Pantlind Hotel for a bit, and Mrs. Murphy was also Elmer's sister. Elmer lived with the two for a bit in their apartment, where he became familiar with James Minnema and started to buy illegal liquor from him.

According to the Murphys, the couple had gone with James the night before the murder to Herbert Sandy's place to purchase a gallon and a half of moonshine. They had loaned James five dollars to help make the purchase. Their story was confirmed when Herbert Sandy was arrested for bootlegging. Herbert had known James and admitted he had sold him booze. It was also learned that the three men who had first discovered James's body were Herbert, and brothers Andrew and Lloyd Centill. Herbert had come to James's apartment to collect ten dollars he owned him and to gather up empty liquor bottles to reuse. As they were already on the wrong side of the law, they had skipped out of the apartment building and didn't wait around for the police to show up and make statements.

Elmer Matthews was contacted in Missouri by police. He shockingly agreed to come back to Grand Rapids and willingly confessed. It had been festering on his conscience. He said he had indeed arrived to James's apartment by taxi that night. Elmer told James that night he had paid some of his rent with the money James had given him earlier to go out and buy booze with. Angry, James started to attack Elmer. He was furious Elmer had taken his money like that and said they would go together and buy more. Once outside, James and Elmer got into a physical fight over the spent money. The masher was on the ground, and Elmer used it to attack James. He knew he had thumped James hard with the wooden tool but never thought it would cause his death. James staggered back into his apartment, and Elmer went back to the waiting taxi.

Elmer was sentenced on January 2, 1922, and told the judge, "Well, sir, I've got this to say: it was just a drunken row. He [Minnema] was violating the law himself. I did not have much money to buy booze with. He helped me to get into trouble, helped to buy the booze. If it were not for that I would not be in this trouble." The judge heard this as Elmer trying to place the blame on someone else. Elmer was sentenced to life in prison in solitary confinement at Marquette.

As he prepared to go to prison, Elmer had two Bibles. One he wanted sent to his sister in Missouri, and the other one he wanted sent to Inez Buskirk in Coopersville. Any place where there was a blank space, Elmer had written notes to her. The notes were "a frantic plea for her to stick to him." Elmer said, "I do not blame her for telling the truth, I'm glad she did it. From now on, I shall live a Christian life." He also told the courts the Murphys had nothing to do with the murder. Pieces of his life came out in the courtroom. He had been born and raised in Missouri in a well-to-do family. His father had been a farmer. He married, but his wife died on February 7, 1918, from tuberculosis, and his two-year-old son, William, died just a few weeks later on March 11 from cerebral meningitis. He had been drafted for World War I but was sent home from camp after a couple weeks because of "fallen arches." He was then sent to Fort Dodge in Iowa for "limited service" and mustered out at Fort Wayne in Detroit. He worked as a mechanic for a while in Detroit and then found himself in Jackson, where he met Inez.

Inez had left her husband, and she and her baby daughter, Lillian, moved with Elmer to Grand Rapids, where he was able to support them for a bit. But a promised winter job in a gravel pit fell through, and Inez found herself looking for work to make ends meet. Elmer had also developed a heavy drinking problem at some point; it's possible that's why he couldn't keep a steady job. Inez found work in Coopersville at Ed McGhan's grading camp.

After his fight with James, Elmer saw the headlines in the paper the next morning, reporting that James had been murdered. Elmer had never intended to kill him. It was just "a drunken row," like he had told the judge, and he was scared. He told Inez what had happened and said he was going to go back home to Missouri. Elmer stated he was not guilty of murder; he thought manslaughter at best because he never intended to kill James.

Ironically, the Detective Doyle who discovered the clue that led to the arrest of Elmer Matthews was suspended from duty after having been on the force for twenty years. It was discovered he was drunk when he escorted Elmer to Marquette Prison on January 7, 1922. He was reinstated on February 1 and promised that something like that would never happen again. So much for Prohibition!

Chapter 6

The Tragedy of Charlie Pohlman

On Friday, April 10, 1903, William Pohlman glanced nervously at the time. It was past six o'clock. The sun would be setting in a couple hours, and his seven-year-old son, Charlie, only one month away from his eighth birthday, had never come home after school. Charlie's mother was especially worried. He was a good boy and never did anything to upset his parents. It wasn't like him to not come home. William wondered if his son was hiding outside somewhere, scared of getting in trouble because he hadn't come home for dinner. They gave it some more time, but after the family had finished eating and Charlie still hadn't come through the door, Charlie's mother, Nellie, urged her husband to go out and look for him, as she couldn't. She had suffered a stroke recently at the young age of twenty-six and was paralyzed as a result. She was extremely worried, and something didn't feel right to her. William put on his coat and went out into the cool spring evening. The skies above showed signs that rain was on the horizon, and the sun had already set. William walked down the street, looking down alleyways, calling Charlie's name and scanning the people walking on the streets. It was now after 9:00 p.m., and William was really starting to wonder what had happened to his son. As he continued down the street, two women passed him, and he happened to catch a few words of their conversation. Their faces were grim as they walked past, and he heard them talking about a little boy who had been found and how tragic it was.

William headed in the direction the women had come from and saw a large group of people huddled around something on the ground. Lanterns

The Pohlman family home on Gold Street. *From* Grand Rapids Herald.

had been set up in the area for light. As William got closer, he could see there was a body on the ground. The body had on a little red sweater. William recognized that sweater as the one his son had been wearing that morning when he left for school. His stomach lurched, and he pushed through the crowd and told the police who he was. He looked down and saw the lifeless body of his little son Charlie. Not only was his son dead, but his head had been severed from his body. When William asked what had happened, the police shrugged and suggested that Charlie had been playing along the train tracks, which so many little boys did, and he must have jumped over the tracks at the wrong moment.

Albert Bowen and his wife had walked through the train yards on their way home and were the first ones to discover the boy's body on the tracks around 8:45 p.m. They alerted the policeman in the area immediately. It seemed like an open and shut case and just another unfortunate and tragic accident—until William pointed out a mark that looked like a hole on Charlie's forehead. William asked the police and the undertakers at the

Adorable Charlie Pohlman holding his hat. *From* Grand Rapids Herald.

scene what had caused such a mark. They said it was probably just a result of the train running over the poor boy's head. That answer was too easy; William wasn't satisfied with it and asked the coroner to inspect it more closely during the autopsy.

Officer VanDine didn't feel that Charlie's death was an accident and spoke up. He didn't like the way the body was found casually laying over the tracks, as if the little boy had just laid down and used the metal railing as a pillow and just fell asleep in a noisy, dirty train yard. If Charlie had been carelessly playing among the trains as the police suggested, Van Dine felt like the body would have been more mangled or in a different position than the relatively peaceful one it had been found in. Once his suspicions were suggested to others, it was determined that an investigation would be opened. The police tried to gather evidence from the area Charlie was found in, but before they could fully take in the whole space, the rain that had been threatening came down in a torrential downpour that went on all weekend. Any evidence that the police could have found helpful, such as blood or footprints, was washed away with the April rains. All the police had from the scene was a bloodstained feed sack. There had been more blood toward the bottom of the sack, making the police speculate that someone had carried Charlie's body to the tracks in the bag. Other than that one clue, the police had nothing to work with. Forensics didn't yet exist like it does today, so sending the bloodied bag to a crime lab to be analyzed was not even possible. A logo on the bag was covered up with blood and grease, making it hard to read.

William went home and told his frail wife what had happened. She was beside herself. Charlie wasn't known to play by the train yards ever. Both parents hoped that the police would do all they could to discover how something so awful could have happened to such a well-liked and wonderful little boy. The police were already asking for anyone who may have any information, no matter how small, to step forward and share it, but nothing was coming in.

Two days later, newspaper headlines read "Mystery of Death...Not Killed by Cars!" During Charlie's autopsy, Coroner Hilliker inspected the hole in Charlie's forehead that William had pointed out, and what the coroner found shocked him. The hole hadn't been caused by the rail cars, as originally thought. Dr. Hilliker extracted a .22-caliber bullet from the little boy's brain. He was also able to tell that Charlie had been dead when his body was placed on the railroad tracks. There was now a whole other side to the story, not just one of a little boy carelessly playing too close to trains and dying by accident. The .22-caliber bullet told another story— one of murder.

THE INVESTIGATION BEGINS

The people of Grand Rapids were stricken with sorrow over the tragedy of an innocent seven-year-old boy being killed and thrown on the tracks. The whole thing was horrifying to people, and whoever had done such an awful act had to be found and punished for their disgusting crime. It was obvious that whoever had shot the boy had hoped the train running over his body would destroy the evidence and forever excuse them of their wrongdoing.

Detectives Joseph Smith and Sherman Jakeway, two of the best detectives in Grand Rapids at the time, took it upon themselves to get to the bottom of the mystery as quickly as possible. The *Grand Rapids Press* was already describing the unfolding story as "one of the darkest murder mysteries in the history of the city." The first order of business was to interview anyone who may have seen Charlie alive that day and trace his steps. Their first clue came from a deliveryman named Lewis Swartz, who had seen Charlie playing with some boys he recognized, Henry and Otto Hasse. The boys were questioned right away and were even brought in to the detectives by their father, Adolf Hasse, who suspected his boys knew something. But the boys said they knew nothing, had a good alibi and were excused. Charlie's schoolteacher told the detectives that Charlie had stayed a little late after school to help her clean up the room and left around 4:00 p.m. After school, he headed over to Joseph Pitsch's barn, where Joseph would let Charlie help him groom his horses.

The detectives lined up as many kids as they could to interview who knew Charlie, were in his class at school or had seen him at some point on April 10. None of the kids seemed to have any useful information. On the night of Charlie's death, a Polish man dragged his son to the scene and forced him to look at Charlie. He asked his son if he had known him. The boy just looked down at his feet and shrugged. His father started to wave his finger in his son's face and yelled at him in Polish. The detectives thought maybe this boy had known something, but when they figured out who the Polish family was, there was no valuable information to glean from them either.

Interviewing the children had turned out to be more of an obstacle than the detectives had bet on. Many of the parents had warned their children not to speak to the police or tell them anything for fear that their kids would get involved in a murder mystery. It was an age when circumstantial evidence could easily put someone behind bars or wrongly incriminate someone and damage a reputation, and parents didn't want their kids to even get involved. When it came to interviewing the kids, Smith and Jakeway had to be delicate and were beyond frustrated with the lack of results. The *Grand Rapids Press* wrote, "The detectives cannot use the severity that would characterize their investigation were they dealing with the average crook." These were kids, not the degenerates the detectives were used to questioning.

The detectives were running into brick wall after brick wall. One thing was certain for the two men: the crime had not been done intentionally. They were positive that whatever happened that day had been an accident, but how it had happened and who was hiding the secret was what they couldn't figure out.

On Wednesday, April 15, 1903, the *Grand Rapids Press* offered a $100 reward for anyone who could help solve the mystery. William Pohlman and his wife were beyond thankful for how helpful and supportive the newspaper was being to help bring the case to a swift close. Charlie had been on everyone's minds and was part of the daily conversation. Of course, the city was wild with rumors, and gossip was flying off the lips of residents who tried to figure out who had committed the awful crime. This wasn't just another murder caused by a drunken brawl, a burglary or a spat between men turned lethal. This was the unnecessary killing of an adorable seven-year-old boy whose body was further mangled by a train after his death. No one wanted to see this case fall into the books as unsolved.

Wild theories and opinions surfaced around the town, one involving the historical figure of William Tell, whom the kids had learned about in school just a week before Charlie's death. The William Tell legend says that he had to shoot an apple while it sat on top of his son's head to save his life. Citizens theorized that maybe one of the older boys put an apple on Charlie's head, tried their best impersonation of William Tell and failed. Another rather amusing scenario was that a woman committed the crime. The *Grand Rapids Press* stated, "A woman carried away in a moment of passion might grab the rifle of her son and shoot the little fellow, who might have been the unconscious cause of her wrath. It would be the most natural act of a woman to try and hide the results of her anger and any woman might have placed the body on the tracks without attracting undue attention." Neither of these scenarios made an impression on the police. They just proved how desperate the search was becoming.

The $100 reward had motivated people to fine-tune their memories in an effort to solve the mystery and take home the reward cash. John Rohn was one of the first to come forward and stated he had been walking home from his job at the Livingston Hotel and always walked past the train yards. On the night of April 10 when he left work, he said he had heard a gunshot go off by the trains. He didn't think much about it because people shot guns in the train yards quite often for target practice, but just before he heard the shot, he had seen a group of boys running around playing. John said the tallest one of the kids was swinging a sack over his head, playfully chasing after the other kids. After the gunshot, he heard piercing yells that didn't sound like happy children anymore. John claimed he heard one of the boys yell, "You shot Charlie…or Willie!" He wasn't quite sure what name he had heard.

John headed in the direction of the voices to see if something had gone wrong and saw the tallest boy appear to be wiping his hands on the sack. The boys saw John and took off running at full speed. He watched them for a while to see if they went into a familiar building, but they just kept running. He figured if one of them was hurt, they weren't hurt too badly if they were able to run that fast. John walked away from the train yards and continued on his way home.

With the new addition of John's story, the detectives were really starting to believe Charlie's death was accidental. It's possible the boys had been playing with real guns in the train yard and Charlie had been killed. They also believed it was possible the little boy could have fallen dead onto the tracks, with his head resting on the metal. The other boys freaked out and left the body there, later to be run over by an oncoming train. The sack they were playing with may have been used to wipe off some of Charlie's blood. But just when the detectives finally felt like they had something to work with, John's story didn't hold up under scrutiny. The detectives determined that from where John had reported seeing the kids, there was no way for him to have heard any voices, let alone actually be able to distinguish specific words. Whether John was just going after the reward money or had genuinely seen some kids playing in the area and heard a gun go off, it wasn't useful information for the investigation.

Barnhardt Rapp admitted to the detectives that he had seen two boys carrying a smaller boy between them at about 6:15 p.m. on that Friday, April 10. He claimed they were maybe around ages thirteen and fifteen and were running with the boy and occasionally taking breaks to catch their breath. Another man claimed he had been sitting inside his home looking out one of his windows that faced the train yards and thought he saw four boys trying to pull a wagon with something in it through the loose gravel. He watched them, entertained by their struggle. They were too far away for the man to see any good details about what was in the wagon or what the boys looked like.

Meanwhile, the police had done a good job of piecing together Charlie's steps after school let out at 3:15 p.m. Charlie was so well known on the west side of Grand Rapids that the police were able to track his movements up until 6:15 p.m. He had stayed behind and helped his teacher clean up. After that, he went to help Joseph Pitsch take care of his horses in his barn behind his meat market store. Then, Charlie ran off to play with his friend Otto Hasse. Adolf, Otto's father, saw the boys playing and, driving up to them in his wagon, asked his son Otto to get in. Charlie followed, and the three rode off a little ways down the street. The wagon stopped, and the boys jumped out and started to play again. That was around 5:00 p.m. At 6:00 p.m., the deliveryman Lewis Swartz asked Charlie if he wanted a ride home, which he declined. At 6:10 p.m., Charlie was once again seen playing with Otto and his brother Henry near Joseph Pitsch's barn. That was the last time anyone saw Charlie Pohlman alive.

The train yard workers had some of the most valuable information to give. Albert Gunn, a car checker who worked in the yards the night of April 10, stated that Charlie's body had to have been placed on the rails sometime between 7:40 and 7:55 p.m; he suspected 7:50. He had inspected both sides of the train at 7:40 and would have seen a body on the track. Everything was clear, and the train pulled out on schedule at 7:55 p.m. Albert had been startled by a boy who popped up out of nowhere from under a train in the same location where Charlie was later found. He yelled at the kid to get away from the trains, as it was dangerous, and the kid scurried off quickly.

No matter how convincing they were during their interviews, the detectives kept casting suspicious eyes on eleven-year-old Otto and fourteen-year-old Henry Hasse, the boys who were last seen with Charlie. Their father, Adolf, did tell police that he owned a .22-caliber rifle the boys played with, but he had taken it away from them. The Hasse boys were considered a little "ruff around the edges." Their father owned a saloon on Jefferson Street, and the family lived above it. The boys spent much of their time in the saloon, and both had jobs at Smith's Opera House on Market Avenue, which was not the classy place the name would imply to a modern reader. While a beautiful building inside and out, Smith's was considered a "low variety theater" and featured comedians, boxing matches, minstrel shows and the ever-popular burlesque dancers.

Their jobs at Smith's had originally been the boys' rock-solid alibi. They said after dinner, they went straight to the theater, and other workers there seemed to uphold the alibi, saying the boys had been at the theater ready to work around 6:30 p.m. Of course, this meant that there was no way they could have put the body on the tracks at the appointed time. Not seeing any other option, Detectives Smith and Jakeway decided to take one more stab at getting the boys to confess if they knew anything, and this time, they had one piece of very incriminating evidence. They didn't want the young brothers to be the killers, but deep down, they knew they had solved the mystery.

On the night of April 29, 1903, Jakeway and Smith were waiting for the brothers when they got done with their work shift just before midnight. The men told the boys they were being arrested and quietly brought them to the police station, where they let them sweat it out overnight. The boys cried all night, and it was hard for the men working at the jail to not feel bad.

It was decided to first interview them separately. Henry, the oldest, was brought in first. Henry, although obviously scared and shaking, still stuck to his old story that he knew nothing. That's when the detectives placed Charlie's blue golf cap down on the desk. Henry's eyes widened in horror at the sight of the hat, as if the ghost of Charlie had just appeared in the room.

The detectives then played the classic game of "good cop, bad cop." Detective Jakeway outright accused Henry of killing Charlie deliberately, while Smith played the "good cop," suggesting that it had been an accident. The cops went back and forth with Henry, and finally Jakeway pointed at the boy and said, "You killed him. Now, how did he fall?" Henry broke down in tears and started to describe the whole sad tale from start to finish, telling the cops every detail they had wanted to know. Because the person describing the gruesome details was a fourteen-year-old boy, the two men started to feel their emotions get the best of them and could only feel sorry for Henry. The *Grand Rapids Press* later recapped the success story of the detectives in an article on May 30, 1903, and wrote, "The detectives said afterwards that the statement of the boy gave them the sensation of an icy hand closing upon their hearts. They forgot all the triumph of closing up the tiresome case in their feeling of compassion for the poor, little evil doers."

Henry said they had invited Charlie to come into their house and play with them. They started to play Wild West, and Henry pulled out a "squirrel rifle" and started aiming it at the other boys, acting as if they were the wild Indians and he the brave cowboy. Aiming the gun at Charlie, Henry pulled the trigger, not realizing the gun was loaded. In one quick second, the bullet went straight into Charlie's forehead and he fell to the ground, dead. The Hasse boys panicked. They huddled together in a corner of the room and just stared at the lifeless little boy on their floor. Henry's first thought was that they would be hanged for what they had done. Knowing they were in the worst trouble of their young lives, they quickly put their heads together on how they could cover up what had just happened. It was Henry's idea to put the body on the track, and he made his little brother swear that if they did this, he would never tell a soul. Otto promised, and the two got busy conspiring.

Henry ran and grabbed a burlap bag from Joseph Pitsch's barn to put Charlie in. While Otto kept an eye out for their parents, Henry got Charlie's body outside unnoticed and placed it behind a shed. They ran back inside. Dinner was ready, and the boys ate quickly and said they had to get to the theater for work. Once outside, the boys placed Charlie in a toy wagon and got him to the Lake Shore train yards, where they placed his body on the tracks, hoping the train would take care of the rest. The detectives asked them how they covered up the blood, but Henry said that Charlie had barely bled in the house. A few drops had fallen onto the staircase as they were getting him outside, and when questioned about the spots by their mother, the boys told her a stray dog with an injured paw had followed them home. The detectives had caught their little criminals, but now there was a whole other issue at hand: how to punish children for such a gruesome act.

When the story got out, people were shocked that two children had outsmarted the police for so long and had the audacity to do what they did. The *Grand Rapids Press* wrote, "The affair reads like a page from a nickel novel. And that, it appears, is just what it was, with Henry and Otto Hasse simply emulating criminals of whom they had read." The paper didn't look sympathetically on the Hasse brothers at all, stating that normal "healthy-minded boys" would have notified adults of what they had done by accident. Henry admitted that he got the idea to put the body on the tracks from crime and mystery novels he had read.

After a couple days, the boys were allowed to go home. Prosecuting attorney William B. Brown searched and searched the law books for something that would allow a proper punishment for children, but he couldn't find anything that would fit. This was an entirely new and difficult thing to tackle, as the guilty were young kids and not grown adults. The whole thing was totally understood to be an accident, but because the idea of juvenile crime was so new in the courts and law books at the time, there was nothing Brown could do but release the boys. The first juvenile court in the United States had just been established in Cook County, Illinois, a few years prior in 1899, with funding provided by Edith Rockefeller McCormick, but Michigan did not have one in place yet. All the prosecutor could do was turn the boys over to their father for punishment.

Adolph Hasse was ashamed and heartbroken over the whole affair. He admitted that the boys were growing up in a bad home in the saloon and that their mother didn't seem to care about what they were doing. He said he would see about sending the boys to the reform school in Lansing, but the courts had no legal say about what he chose to do with the boys.

This didn't sit well with the citizens of Grand Rapids at all. Justice didn't feel served. While people were relieved that the "west side murder," as some called it, had been solved, there was still a sour taste left behind. In a letter to the editor in the *Grand Rapids Press* on May 6, 1903, the author suggested that if the son of prosecutor William Brown had been murdered, he would have looked and looked through the laws until something could have been used for punishment. The author, Frank Carpenter, didn't agree that the boys should just be "let off the hook" because of their age. The sentiment in the letter and in the city was that they did the crime, and they must pay for it.

The boys found themselves becoming ostracized. Even Adolf was punished. On May 18, 1903, he was refused a liquor license for his saloon, as were many others in the city, but there was probably more prejudice against him because of his sons' recent crime. It was clear to many who had been refused license renewals that "favoritism" had been shown. Old playmates of Henry and Otto ignored the boys and excluded them from their activities. Parents didn't want their children anywhere near the boys. They were coldly stared at by people as they passed by them on the streets. The world wasn't a kind place anymore for the Hasse boys. They felt the sting of what they had done with every ice-cold glance that came their way. Perhaps this punishment was worse than any amount of time spent walled up in a jail cell.

Chapter 7

The Mysterious Death of Mina Dekker

It was just another workday on Friday, March 4, 1938, for Mina Dekker. Mina was a nineteen-year-old stenographer at the Behr-Manning Corporation that specialized in abrasives, located on the third floor of the Judd Building at 64 Ionia Avenue. The manager, Charles Blackford, and his son asked Mina to take an early lunch that day so someone would be in the building when they took off for their lunch, leaving her alone in the building while they were away. Only the first and third floors out of four were being used at the time; the first floor was occupied by the Manufacturers Supply Company.

Ray Peters, a thirty-eight-year-old shoe repairman who owned a store on Jefferson Street, stopped into Behr-Manning during the lunch hour to pick up some supplies. According to his story, he came in and couldn't find anyone available, so he sat down and waited. The place was quiet. He got up and looked around when he thought he heard a woman moaning. The sound was coming from the storeroom. On the floor of the room lay the body of Mina. A large amount of blood was pooled under her, and by the looks of it, her head had been brutally bashed. Ray ran down to the first floor in search of help, where he found some men, including Calvin Deblaey, playing cards around a table. Calvin and the other men ran upstairs to see the girl, and Calvin called the police. The police got there quickly and rushed Mina to the hospital but with no success. She died three hours later at St. Mary's Hospital. Her skull had been fractured in five places. Mina had probably tried to defend herself from her attacker, as the pinky on her right hand was also broken. No murder weapon was found

Mina Dekker's senior photo. *Courtesy of David Schock, PhD.*

at the scene, but the marks on her head suggested a hammer had been used. She had been hit so hard in the same spot that it caused a piece of her skull to be laying on the floor next to her.

The obvious people to interview first were the men who had been at the Manufacturers Supply Company on the first floor. None of them had heard anything out of the ordinary. Ray Coby said he had heard the elevator move but hadn't seen anyone enter the building that he was aware of. Seventeen-year-old Herbert Banning was a Western Union messenger and had stopped into the third floor shortly before the murder had taken place. He was the last person to report seeing Mina alive, which meant the crime had happened sometime between 12:50 p.m., when she received the telegram from Herbert, and 1:30 p.m., when she was found by Ray Peters.

John Schafer had been engaged to Mina several weeks prior to the murder. They had dated for a year and were going to wait to marry when they had enough money saved up, but they had a "falling out." Schafer felt that if "she had not been killed, they probably would have hooked back up." He was attending business school and was in class during the murder, which could be verified, so he was off the hook as a possible suspect and never questioned again.

Mina's funeral was held three days later on March 7 at the family home on Oakland Avenue. Later, she was taken to the Fifth Reformed Church, and over one thousand people gathered inside, including many "curiosity seekers." Police camped out at the funeral, observing the crowd for anyone suspicious. Mina was buried in Restlawn Cemetery.

THE SEARCH FOR THE KILLER

The murder shocked Grand Rapids, and the story gained national attention. There didn't seem to be any reason for the senseless and cruel act. The police had nothing to go on at first, and Police Chief Frank O'Malley stated, "Someone out there must know something! Blood on a shirt, anything!" He told the public the police would be searching the rooming houses and seedy parts of Grand Rapids and that "every degenerate known to police will face questioning," assuming that only known degenerates commit heinous crimes. O'Malley felt the crime could have only been committed by a "fiend," and "without a visible motive, we must proceed with that idea in mind. We must assume that the killer knew Mina and was there during the noon hour with her. However, we are not overlooking that the location is one which is frequented by transients," meaning tramps and street people.

The year 1938 wasn't starting out to be a good one for the Grand Rapids Police Department. This was the second murder of the year that didn't have a motive. The other murder was the coldblooded killing of Marinus Lindhout, a sixty-three-year-old grocer of 423 Jefferson Avenue, at 12:30 a.m. on February 11, 1938. Marinus was shot in the chest, and police figured it was a holdup but discovered nothing had been taken from the store, not even cash.

Calvin Deblaey, one of the men who had been playing cards on the first floor when the murder took place, was a prime suspect from the beginning. Calvin was no stranger to the police and had been under investigation in the past for stealing money but was never convicted. He had also "reported himself the victim of a hold up," saying he had been robbed at Oak Hill Cemetery. In reality, he was trying to "cover his gambling losses" and had never been robbed. Some rumors said Calvin had a bit of history with Mina different from the others who were in the building that day, as he had tried to date her. She hadn't been interested in him and turned him down and had actually expressed a dislike for the man. It was rumored that Calvin had tried to talk to her that Friday morning, but it's not known if Calvin ever confirmed those rumors.

After a few suspects were taken in for questioning and let go, having no useful information, it was announced on March 11 that twenty-seven-year-old Calvin was being held and was asked to take a truth serum test but had refused and wanted to speak to a member of the clergy. The clergyman reported that Calvin had not confessed anything to him and didn't "shed any new light on the subject." He told the priest he had been at Uptown

Recreation "gambling" during the lunch hour. Calvin had also taken two polygraph tests before the truth serum was suggested: one on March 8 and another on March 11. The state lie detector expert, Lieutenant Harold Mulbar, said he had been incredibly nervous during the first one, and he suspected "he had something on his mind." Both tests were "inconclusive," but when asked the question, "Did you kill Mina Dekker?" Calvin's "no" seemed to be genuine, according to the test.

Truth serum had been experimented with for a couple decades in the 1920s and '30s. It was being used more and more by police departments. It seemed a "scientific" means to gain answers but, in fact, did not have a proven track record of success. The truth serum being used was the chemical scopolamine, derived from plants and largely given to women in labor in the first half of the twentieth century. The drug wasn't necessarily a painkiller but got rid of the *memory* of pain. It would put people in what was called a "twilight sleep," and during numerous experiments with it, it was also thought to get people to tell the truth when asked a question. The emerging science of forensics utilized the drug in many early criminal cases, but the test results couldn't usually be relied on. Calvin announced on March 12 that he would take the truth serum injection at Lansing after being held for three hours with prosecutor Fred Searl, who talked him into taking the test.

The serum was administered by Dr. L.M. Snyder, the medical examiner for the state police. He asked the questions, "What is your name? Age? Did you use a hammer? Where did you hide the weapon? Did you use a club?" Dr. Snyder felt that Calvin answered the questions honestly and didn't gain a confession. He was released from police custody the same day. This had been the first case in Michigan where truth serum was used to determine an outcome that held up in court.

Police could not confirm any of Calvin's movements on the day Mina was killed. He told police he drove his truck to the rear of the Judd Building on Friday at 1:00 p.m. Before entering the building, he decided to get a cup of coffee at a nearby restaurant. He told police his stomach had been bothering him, so he "passed on lunch" that day but decided he should pick up a cup of coffee before coming back to work so at least he had something in his stomach. He returned to the office at 1:15 p.m. and joined in on the card game with the other employees. At the very least, no one could account for his whereabouts during a portion of the time it was believed the murder had happened.

With Calvin's release, the police were frustrated and felt like they had been brought back to the start again. "We have little or nothing to work on," said Police Chief O'Malley. "Frankly, I don't know what the next step will be. Apparently we will have to be lucky and get a break."

MINA'S PERSONAL LIFE

To help further the case, the police tried to investigate Mina's personal life and background to see if there was anything that could expose a motive that would prompt murder. Details of Mina's personal life trickled into the newspapers. No one had anything bad to say about her. She was a beautiful young woman who sang in her church choir. Her family was Dutch immigrants who were honest and hardworking people.

A sensational headline from the *Grand Rapids Press* read "Slain Mina Dekker Took Secret Fear to Grave: Mother and Girlfriend Knew of Her Terror but Not What It Was." The night before Mina was killed, she had been scared of something. Mina had gone to a wedding shower for one of her close friends, Mary Kosten. While talking to friends at the party, she told them she was scared to walk home alone that night. She asked Mary if she would escort her home and she would fill her in on why she was scared, but Mary felt it would be rude to leave her shower. She regretted not walking her home later, knowing that she might have learned some information that could have helped solve the mystery. The night before she was killed, "she was afraid of something…something was on her mind," said Mina's mother when she was questioned. For police, "this strengthened the notion that it was someone who knew Mina who had killed her."

By March 30, the police thought they had two new possible suspects, but they were long shots. Police Chief O'Malley had been notified by Detroit police that they had detained an eighteen-year-old man who had arrived with scratches on his face shortly after Mina's murder. The man admitted he had been in Grand Rapids the day of Mina's slaying. The young man came back from his Grand Rapids trip excitedly talking about the murder. His mother became concerned and asked the police to investigate. The man's alibi was confirmed, however, and he was released from police custody. He had been working on a farm in Cascade. His scratches were just from cats.

The other man, Dirk DePung, had sent in a pair of bloody pants to get cleaned just four days after the murder. It is probably not the best time to send in your bloodstained clothing while a nation is looking for a suspected killer on the loose. The man was jailed and held for questioning. The pants had already been cleaned though, and the state police chemist wasn't able to trace any blood on them. The man lived near the Judd Building, where the murder had taken place. The fact that the pants were sent to an address other than the man's home made the police suspect him. Supposedly, the man's wife could not pay the cleaning bill, so she told him to send the pants to another house, trying to get someone else to pay the bill. The bloodstains turned out to be from an injured horse.

A MURDER UNSOLVED

While the majority suspected Calvin as the murderer, Ray E. Peters, the shoe repairman who first found Mina, was asked to take a lie detector test. Peters was never really suspected of the crime by the police, but rumors around town suggested otherwise just because he had been the first to find her body. To put those rumors to bed, Ray agreed to take a test. According to his grandchildren in a documentary on the website "Delayed Justice," he paid out of pocket to take two more polygraph tests just to prove to people he didn't have anything to do with the killing. Finding her body affected Ray for the rest of his life.

The case was handed down through the years from one investigator to the next. It was always believed that the killer was still out there for decades and the case could possibly still be solved. Sergeant John Robinson got interested in the case when he joined the detective bureau of the major case team in 1977. In the "Delayed Justice" film, he said he contacted Calvin Deblaey to ask him about the case in the 1980s. By this point, Calvin was seventy-six, and when John finally managed to catch him on the phone, Calvin said he had nothing to say and that he had been cleared of the case. John told him, "There comes a time when you're going to be meeting your maker," but he never heard from Calvin again. John had been the last investigator to talk to Calvin.

While Calvin had always been a prime suspect to the authorities, there really wasn't solid evidence to suggest he had committed the crime, only that he had lied about his whereabouts that day because he had been gambling. If Calvin had done the crime, why would he stick around the building, call the police and stay living in the area for the rest of his life? Could the police have been so convinced it was Calvin all these years that they didn't continue to look elsewhere?

The front cover of *True Detective* magazine, November 1938. *Used with permission from www. truecrimelibrary.com.*

When Detective Breen retired from the force in 1987, he told a *Grand Rapids Press* reporter, "I am completely convinced in my own mind that I know the identity of the person who killed her. I am as certain of it as I am that my name is Frank Breen, but because of certain peculiar circumstances, which I cannot divulge here, it has been impossible so far to accumulate enough evidence against this person to ensure a conviction." He went on to say, "Her case has not been and never should be marked closed until her slayer is dead or behind bars." It's not known who he thought the killer was.

To this day, it remains Grand Rapids' oldest and most mysterious unsolved homicide and is still considered an open case. Whoever did the awful deed is probably dead by now, but hopefully someday the truth can still be learned. In an interview, Adrian Dekker, Mina's younger brother, told Dr. David Schock, who has researched the murder extensively, that their parents had said, "He may get away with it here, but he won't get away in front of God."

Chapter 8

The Day Henry Bedford Went Mad

Forty-three-year-old Henry Bedford was an intelligent and somewhat handsome man who had moved around a lot in his life, taking on different jobs in Illinois, Ohio and Michigan in the public school systems and always moving up the pay scale as he did it. Before he landed a job in Michigan as the principal of the Turner Public School in Grand Rapids, he had been a textbook salesman. He was a smooth talker and made a decent income, but being a successful salesman didn't equate to having success in other areas of his life. Henry had separated from his wife of twenty-one years, Mabel, and had been living on his own. She filed for divorce in 1932 and moved to Tennessee with their two daughters, Faith and Joy.

Henry had owned a second house in Grand Rapids that he rented out, and when his wife commenced with the divorce proceedings, Henry had no other option but to sell the house he and his family had been living in and move in with his renters, Carl and Maggie Bengert, and their young son and baby boy. Everything went downhill for the Bengerts when Henry moved in.

Freshly divorced and back on the market, Henry took a liking to Maggie. She was young and attractive, and Henry was tall, handsome and easy to talk to. Maggie's husband, Carl, was a furniture upholsterer and was struggling to find steady work to support his family. From the start, Carl hadn't gotten along well with Henry when he moved into the home. He noticed the way Henry paid extra attention to his wife and didn't appreciate it. Carl knew his wife was flattered by the man, and the whole situation was putting a strain on their marriage. Eventually, Carl learned his wife had had an affair with

Henry. Carl and Henry got into a huge argument, and even though Carl was living in the house, Henry owned it and told Carl to leave. Maggie agreed with Henry and told her husband it would be best if he stayed away for a few days to let everyone calm down. He left the house, angry and hurt, and stayed with family in the area.

On April 6, 1933, Maggie's sister called up Carl and told him to go by the house, as Maggie was ready to talk to him. Carl felt better and was looking forward to sorting things out and seeing his children again. Carl headed over to the house and knocked on the door, but no one answered. He knocked again. Nothing. He tried the door, but it was locked. Something felt wrong. Walking across the street to a neighbor's house, he asked for an axe and invited the neighbor to come over and help him pry open the door, as he was worried. As Carl hacked the door and kicked it open, he was greeted by the body of Henry Bedford laying over two kitchen chairs. The gas from the oven was turned on full blast, and the fumes in the kitchen were noxious. Henry was unconscious but still alive. The two men grabbed his body and threw him outside on the front porch.

Carl was in a panic. What had happened? Where were his wife and kids? Why was Henry found trying to kill himself? Carl raced through the house looking through the rooms. Dashing upstairs, barely touching a step, he opened the door to his bedroom and found his wife. She had been strangled and was lying dead on their bed. Carl's world was caving in around him. He grabbed his wife and tried to see if there was any life inside her, but there was nothing. It was too late. The police were called immediately, but Carl still hadn't located his two boys: Carl Jr., who was eight, and his three-month-old baby boy, Thalbert. Carl frantically searched and found Thalbert in the last place any sane person would think to look: the oven. The innocent baby had been suffocated from the gas. Carl Jr. was found last outside in the detached garage, strangled and killed the same way his mother had been.

Henry Bedford was dragged into police headquarters unconscious and barely alive. When he came to, he said he had no clue what had happened. He had been eating lunch and didn't remember anything after that. Someone must have wanted to rob the house so they poisoned the milk, causing him to pass out, and then they killed the family.

This story didn't last long, and Henry wasn't stupid. He knew he had been caught and his plan to kill himself along with the family he murdered had failed. The *Grand Rapids Press* reported that "Henry was calm to the degree of coldness throughout the questioning and court routine." Henry told the story of his rampage to the prosecutor. He had offered Carl Jr. a

An antique 1908 postcard of the old Grand Rapids police headquarters. *Author's collection.*

ride to school, and once he got him in the garage, he strangled the boy first with a piece of cord. Not having the boy around to distract him or scream for help, Henry marched back into the house and killed Maggie the same way, strangling her with a piece of cord in her bedroom. By this point, he was so deranged with anger that he grabbed the helpless baby, who couldn't even defend himself, and put him in the oven to suffocate him. He then laid himself down in the kitchen to die from the gas.

The prosecutor asked for more details, and Henry plainly said, "It's too gruesome. I intend to plead guilty so why must I go into those gruesome details." The prosecutor then told him a "sanity commission" would examine him, and Henry flat out said, "Oh, I'm sane all right." He said his mind went into a frenzy when Maggie told him she wasn't interested in pursuing a relationship with him and she was going to mend things with Carl. She had considered her time with Henry just a "fling" but nothing serious. Henry, on the other hand, had planned to propose to Maggie, thinking she would leave her husband. If Henry couldn't have the family, no one would, and that was his only motive. When asked how he could do something so awful, all he could respond with was, "I guess I went mad."

Henry told the prosecutor that "Carl mistreated his wife," and he seemed to display a hatred for Carl on all levels, even saying that Carl owed him money and he still wanted to be paid back. It was ironic that he complained of Carl possibly not treating his wife kindly when the reason his own wife was divorcing him was on grounds of cruelty, as he had tried to choke her and would have possibly killed her if one of his daughters hadn't stepped in and put a stop to it.

Within twenty-four hours, Henry was convicted and sentenced to life in prison. Before he was shipped off to Marquette Prison, police escorted Henry back to the home so he could gather up a few things. As he was changing his clothes at the house, it was reported that he casually pulled a piece of cord out of his pocket and tossed it on his bed like a piece of pocket lint. It appeared to be the same type of cord he had used to strangle Maggie and Carl Jr. The story went national right away, and headlines all over the United States told of the "Demented Principal." When asked to pose for a photo, he resisted at first and then actually posed, holding a pen and tilting his head to the side, not looking directly at the camera. He still wanted to look composed and intelligent, even if the photo was taken because he had just murdered an entire family.

The funeral for the family was held, and Maggie and her two sons were buried in Evansville, Indiana, where a sister and two brothers lived. Henry was sentenced to Marquette for first-degree murder. In 1940, census records revealed he was at the Ionia State Hospital for the Criminally Insane. He died on September 1, 1973, at the age of eighty-four at the Kalamazoo State Hospital.

Chapter 9

The Fiery Temper of Dora Velzy

On the morning of Wednesday, June 7, 1893, Mrs. Lamore suggested to her husband, Charles, that they should go check on their neighbor William Gray at his apartment. She hadn't seen the young man for a few days, and there didn't seem to be any activity in his apartment on Crescent Avenue. Something felt wrong to her. The couple went up to his door and knocked but received no answer. They knocked again and tried to open the door, but it was locked.

Charles looked through the shutters of the window and squinted into the darkness of the apartment. He could make out the shape of William on his bed and could see what looked like a wound in the side of the man's head. The Lamores contacted the coroner, Dr. Locher, who was close by and got to the apartment in a hurry. Together, the men pried the window open and climbed into the small room. The doctor went in first and gasped as he looked around and stated to the Lamores, "There are two of them here and they are very dead."

William's body was naked, lying on his side under the covers. If no one knew any better, one would think the man had just been sleeping. The doctor immediately noticed the hole in William's right temple. Powder marks around the wound let him know the gun had been fired close to his head. Another bullet had been fired into his heart.

The other body in the room was that of twenty-three-year-old Dora Velzy. Dora was described as "a slender brunette" and exceptionally beautiful, catching the eyes of many as she walked down the streets of Grand Rapids.

She had grown up on a farm in Allendale and came to Grand Rapids to find work in homes as a domestic, cooking and cleaning for families. She and William had been dating off and on for three years.

Dora's body was lying on the floor next to William's bed. All she was wearing was a white robe. The *Grand Rapids Press* reported that her "face was smeared with blood that had flowed from a cruel and gaping wound in her right temple." A gunshot wound was found under her chin and another in her right temple. The old papers loved to report on female victims, describing what they were wearing or how they looked. The *Grand Rapids Press* noted that "her features were classic and her long, tapering fingers indicated that she did not toil laboriously." Next to Dora were a .38-caliber revolver and a suicide note. There were five chambers in the gun, and only one bullet remained. When William's body was rolled over, a ladies' wallet was found underneath him containing $10.40. The wallet had belonged to Dora. Her suicide note was reprinted in the paper and read:

> *The reason why I must do this naughty cowardly thing is because I cannot or will not stand it, to be played the way I have been. He thinks it is smart to tell people I am tough, but he never thinks to tell them that he is the cause of every bit of it. If he had never meddled with me, I would have been a nice, happy girl. Now, the people that used to be my friends will not even look at me when they meet me. He does not tell people about stealing my wages every chance he got. I think a fellow that will rob a hired girl of every cent she had ought to be killed. He used to steal my money every chance he possibly could and then deny it. He is too nice to kill, but I do not want to live and be talked about by people just as decent as some of the married women that talk about me, especially Mrs. (the name of a business man's wife is given) who has always been telling people where I worked all she knew about me. My whole life has been one of trouble and hard work and I might as well die now as ever.*
> *Wishing everyone much happiness and good luck.*
> *D.A. Velzy*

As the story hit the newspapers that afternoon, headlines read "Bloody Deed! Murder and Suicide on Crescent Avenue!"

Citizens formed opinions and theories about the crime. Some wondered if it really had been a murder/suicide. It was strange that Dora, being the one to kill William, had two gunshots in her, but perhaps the first shot under the chin didn't kill her right away and she quickly aimed for her temple on the second shot. Some thought that Dora was so pretty that perhaps a jealous suitor had snuck into William's apartment and killed both of them. Others wondered if Dora had gotten pregnant and, out of shame, killed herself and William, but the autopsy put an end to that rumor, proving it not true.

According to Dora's suicide note, she had been frustrated and angry, writing that William had demanded her money for himself and because of him, she was shunned by friends and others around town. If her note was truthful, it was obvious the two had a rocky relationship. The tragedy was news all over the state and was even picked up in newspapers outside Michigan. The *Kalamazoo Gazette* published a slightly different version of Dora's suicide letter. The one line that was different read, "He does not tell people about giving me a disease when I was a young girl or about stealing my wages every chance he got." The *Grand Rapids Press* wrote things very conservatively, and it's possible it deliberately edited that line due to the sensitive nature of the subject in the nineteenth century.

A coroner's inquest was scheduled the day after the bodies were found to determine the official cause of death. The first witness called to the stand was William's fiancée, who hadn't been Dora Velzy. Anna Marie Hetherington was just eighteen years old and looked young. William had been fifteen years older than her at thirty-three years of age. She told the courtroom she met William in January of the same year and he proposed to her a month later in February. She knew that William had dated Dora in the past, but from what she understood, they were done. Anna had made plans to visit with William at "Mrs. McDonald's" place the night before the bodies were discovered. Anna waited and waited, but William never showed up. Mrs. McDonald told her that William had plans of going to Chicago to live and work with his brother and that he was leaving soon. William had never revealed his plans about moving to Anna, and she was shocked and hurried over to his apartment. She couldn't believe that he would just up and leave and not say goodbye to her or explain anything.

Anna knocked on William's door but didn't get an answer. She wondered if he was inside, and curiosity got the best of her. She tried the door, and it was unlocked. This piece of information immediately shed suspicion on her because the doctor and the Lamores said the door had been locked and that's why they pried open the window to get inside, but it was later learned there were in fact two doors into the apartment, and the one Anna had gone to was the open one.

William's place was dark, and Anna walked toward his bedroom and went to open the door. Something on the floor was in her way, but she

An antique postcard of the old courthouse of Grand Rapids. *Author's collection.*

pushed harder and got into the room. She could see a shape in the bed and knew it was William. She gently touched his face, hoping to wake him, but he didn't stir, so she turned around to leave. Her eyes had adjusted to the dark, and she saw the thing that had obstructed the door was a woman dressed in white on the floor. She told the jury that she didn't have any clue they were both dead and "did not know he kept company with any girl." Anna made the innocent assumption that maybe William had been partying at Reed's Lake and this girl had been there and drank too much and needed a place to sleep it off.

Anna hadn't said anything about what she had seen that night because she was a bit embarrassed, having potentially caught her fiancée with a mistress. She was asked how she did not notice that William was dead. She said that it was dark and she had on leather gloves, so when she touched his face, she couldn't feel whether he was hot or cold. Her gloves were inspected, and a small amount of blood was found on them.

The next day, Anna wrote a letter to William and slipped it under his apartment door but didn't mention that she had seen the woman on the floor. She only asked that he "forgive her" for coming into his apartment. She also asked him to "call on her" and let "bygones be bygones," possibly alluding to the fact that she had found him with another woman. She didn't want him to leave without saying goodbye.

Friends and co-workers of Dora were some of the next people called to the stand during the inquest. Bertha Schaubel and Dora had worked at the same house, and Bertha remembered William visiting her at least a couple times a week. Around December 1892, Dora told Bertha that she and William had broken up. Dora said William had desires of moving out of Grand Rapids and she wasn't particularly keen on the idea. This also explains why William had met Anna in January and was engaged a month later. Did William quickly propose to Anna just to make Dora jealous or to prove he didn't need her?

Florence Inwood, "a large, rustic looking girl" who had known Dora for six years, claimed she had a "violent temper." Dora had visited with her the previous Sunday and said some rather strange things. She told Florence she wasn't with William anymore, saying he drank too much and was always jealous of her. She then asked Florence what her opinion was on suicide. "I wouldn't kill myself for the best man living," Florence told her, and Dora replied, "If I killed myself, someone would go with me." Florence noticed a strange look on Dora's face when she said those words and felt something wasn't right with her. She knew that Dora had deeply cared for William, even if she didn't act like it, but she was also very jealous of him at the same time.

William had been a bookkeeper for O'Brien Brothers Undertaking for two years before his death. Patrick O'Brien, William's boss, was asked to go on the witness stand and testify about his former employee's character. Patrick had seen Dora around the office before and said that William was a good person and "wasn't a drinking man." He had been aware of his intentions to move and knew he would be losing a good man. William rented his apartment from Patrick, as it was over his undertaking business. Patrick knew the building and confirmed there were two doors that led into the apartment.

Police interviewed past families Dora had worked for. Many of them remembered she had a "violent and ungovernable temper." She had last worked for Maria Kusterer, who said they had not been happy with her because of her "hasty disposition." Maria also noticed that Dora never seemed to be without money and seemed to have more than "what her wages would have given her. She spent her money freely for what she wanted. She had a fine figure and dressed far better than usual with servant girls." She was told her last day would be Tuesday, June 6, and she needed to pack her trunk and move on. But Maria never saw her on Tuesday morning, and Dora never came to collect her belongings. The family was actually worried that something had happened to her. Maria said that on the previous

Sunday, William had come to the house and talked to Dora on the front porch. Whatever they were talking about appeared serious. He may have been letting her know that he was leaving Wednesday for Chicago and not coming back and wanted to see her one last time.

Another former employer said she had fired Dora for her bad temper and also commented on Dora's style of dress. Dora would wear silk dresses while doing kitchen work instead of more "suitable" dresses like other domestics. "I told her I would prefer her to wear chintz, like the other girls," she stated. The same woman also said that Dora would "fly into a rage on the slightest provocation. No one in the kitchen dared to cross her and I was finally compelled to discharge her."

On Friday, June 9, the inquest continued, and the room was largely attended by the "morbidly curious." The first person on the stand was Henry Velzy, Dora's father. The *Grand Rapids Press* wrote, "When the father of the dead girl was placed on the stand there was a craning of necks and a look of expectancy on every face." The crowd was eager to see what her own father had to say about his daughter. Henry told the room that he was aware Dora had a thing with William for years and he had even advised her not to continue a relationship with him. She shrugged off her father's advice and said it was just for fun and she didn't care that much for him anyways. Henry said his daughter "was self-willed and had a strong temper." He produced a letter Dora had written to her mother. The letter was used to compare the handwriting of Dora's suicide note found in the room when the bodies were discovered. The writing style was identical.

Alfred N. Johns, a neighbor of William's, told the jury he had heard gunshots a couple nights before the bodies were found. After the shots were fired, he thought he heard the sound of a cat whining and figured someone must have killed a stray cat.

DORA'S LETTERS

Henry Velzy, with the help of the police, went to collect his daughter's things from her room at Mrs. Kusterer's. When they opened her trunk, they found a bunch of letters resting on top. The letters were from friends and family, but many were from a man named Will Slater. Her diary was also found and contained entries about him. Will was in the courtroom during the inquest and said he had been engaged to Dora in the past. He had known her and her family since she was little but had been living in Missouri, so he and Dora wrote letters to keep in contact. Dora's and William's writing was so similar that police had to analyze it under closer scrutiny. There was still the slight speculation that a "third and jealous" party was behind William's and Dora's deaths and had staged the killing to look like a murder and suicide. Her last letter from Will Slater was dated March 7, 1893, just three months before her death. The last half of the letter read:

> *I am sorry, Dora, that I could not have seen you more while I was in Michigan, and the way matters stand between us, I suppose it is partly my fault, but it is not all. But I am ready to forget the past if you are. I don't believe there is anything else to say at this time. With best wishes, I remain your true friend,*
> *Wm. E. Slater*

An odd letter that stuck out among the others and was published by the *Jackson Citizen* was from a James Riley of Detroit, even though it was recognized to be William Gray's writing and was on "O'Brien Brothers stationary." Why Gray used a fake name is unknown. The letter seemed a little risqué and read:

> *Miss Dora—You think you are very smart and very cute. You showed it last evening, and if you try it again I will kick your pants good and hard. Now you mind that. Oh, how I do love to spank you. It gives me joy to see you jump around if you do not behave yourself. Tonight there will be a terrible Row in Camp…you think you are smart but I don't believe it is so. I will give you a dam good spanking just before I go. Answer Soon, Kiss me um um.*
> *James Riley*
> *103 Freemont Detroit, Mich.*

There had been suggestions that Dora was a little on the wild side for a lady of her day, and this letter lent some truth to those rumors.

On Friday, June 9, the jury returned a verdict that "Dora Velzy killed Gray and then took her own life while she was laboring under intense mental excitement." The jury felt that the wallet found underneath William's body proved her statement in her letter that he had been taking money from her. This, combined with his leaving town and his treatment of her, Dora, "bordering on insanity," had taken both of their fates into her own hands.

The funerals were held the same day back to back, William's being first. His former co-workers at O'Brien Brothers Undertaking took care of the arrangements, as William didn't seem to be in close contact with his family. Only a few friends showed up to pay their respects, and the funeral was sparsely attended. Anna Hetherington was there the whole time, crying, and didn't want to leave the casket of her dead fiancée. The funeral was conducted by Reverend J.T. Husted, whom William had admired, even though he wasn't a religious man. In his sermon, the reverend suggested that "jealousy is only brought on by great love." Probably not knowing what else to say over such an awful situation, that was the only explanation he could come up with to smooth over the dreadful reason for the funeral.

The only family member to show up was William's brother Charles, who lived in Unionville, located in Michigan's thumb. Charles told people at the funeral he hadn't spoken to his brother in four years, ever since something angered William and he left his family and hadn't bothered to contact them. His mother was old and living in Yale, Michigan, and Charles didn't want her to know about her son's death. It was better she just thought he was alive somewhere in the world. They had another brother living in Chicago and a brother and sister who lived with and took care of their aging mother. Charles had wanted to take the body home with him for burial, but it was too far decomposed. The service had been a closed casket. He was buried in Fairplains Cemetery.

During William's funeral, Dora's coffin sat pushed to the side of the room, waiting. Her family and friends attended her funeral and took her coffin home to be buried in the Allendale Township Cemetery.

Although the coroner's inquest had finished and the cause of death was determined, the police hadn't fully searched her trunk as well as they thought they had. As the police dug deeper through her things, they discovered a box of .32-caliber bullets rolled up in a pair of her many stockings at the very bottom of the trunk. Five bullets were missing from the fifty that were in the box. The bullets were compared with the ones extracted from Dora and William and were identical. Once the bullets were found, there was no doubt in their minds that the verdict was correct. Dora had planned out everything, but it will never be known if she was just a dramatic woman with an extreme temper or if she really had been pushed to her limits by heartbreak and ruin.

Chapter 10

The Reformation of Clara Connolly

When police responded at an apartment building on Commerce Street on August 15, 1907, they were greeted with an awful scene: Clara Connolly holding the bloody, lifeless body of her husband, James, on the front porch. She was frantic, trying to talk to him, telling him that she loved him and asking him if he was in pain. A bullet had punctured his lungs and caused blood to fill them quickly. Clara had been the one who put the bullet there.

Police walked up to the porch and separated Clara from her husband's body. They put James in a wagon to go to the hospital to see if anything could be done for the man other than an autopsy. Clara was put into a patrol wagon and taken down to police headquarters for questioning, and on the way to the station, she passed out cold.

At headquarters, they brought Clara's limp body inside and started to revive her, which involved "repeated dashes of ice water upon her face and breast." Her eyes started to flutter and finally opened. As she looked at her surroundings, the first question from her mouth was, "Where is James?" Officers told her that her husband was dead. She continued to cry out his name as they locked her up in a jail cell.

TWO MARRIAGES GONE WRONG

Clara's past didn't have a kind start. She was born in Saginaw, and her parents died when she was very young. She spent time with her brother and sister in an orphan asylum. At age six, she was adopted by Mary and Thomas Bartlett of Alma, Michigan, where she grew up and married a farmer named George Hodgkinson at the age of seventeen on April 13, 1897. Two years later, they welcomed their first child, Ralph, born on December 16, 1899. On March 1, 1901, their second child, Florence, was born. But even with two children to care for, her relationship with George went south, and it appears she was actually kicked out of the house and the two divorced.

Needing to support herself, Clara started to wait tables at restaurants and cooked at hotels in various cities. She eventually found herself working at the Columbia Hotel in Grand Rapids, where she met James, who also had a job there. The two hit it off well and were married in Grand Rapids on December 11, 1905. James's last name was actually Sweeney, but it was said his parents objected to the marriage because of religious reasons, so he took Clara's birth name of Connolly instead.

From that point, the couple went north and worked various jobs until a couple years later, when they found themselves back in Grand Rapids. According to Clara, their first year of marriage was happy, but after that, James fell into the habit of drinking heavily, and everything went downhill from there. James became lazy and didn't have any ambition to keep a job. They needed money, and James suggested or possibly gave her no choice other than to sell herself and resort to prostitution. It would be quick and easy money. Clara gave in to her husband's hellish plan.

EVERYONE HAS A BREAKING POINT

On August 15, 1907, Clara had her breaking point. She had been sick that day and was feeling awful. She lay down on her bed in their tiny apartment and was awoken by a strange man in her room. He had been sent to see her by James. Knowing what the man wanted but not in any mood to ensure money came in for her husband's drinking habits, she told the stranger to go away and went into the kitchen in search of some salt water to soothe her upset stomach. In the kitchen, she noticed James's standard bottle of whiskey. Out of anger and disgust, she hurled the bottle to the floor, shattering the glass and its contents. She looked down at the shattered pieces, a metaphor of her life.

James had been lurking somewhere outside and knew things weren't going as planned with the gentleman caller he had procured. James went to go back inside the house, but the door was locked. He started to bang on it loudly, yelling for Clara to let him inside. A few neighbors, including the landlady, had noticed a commotion was brewing. Clara yelled from inside, "You'll have to go through the window if you want in." And that's just what James did.

Once inside, he saw his smashed bottle of whiskey. "That's the last bottle of whiskey I'll ever buy for you!" Clara hissed at him. Drunk and enraged, James came at Clara and hit her, knocking her down on the floor and kicking her hard. Clara quickly got up from the floor and ran into the bedroom. James came up from behind, violently grabbed Clara's long blonde hair and threw her back down on the ground.

From her viewpoint on the floor, Clara glanced at the mattress and remembered the revolver that was kept under it. Moving fast, she jammed her hand under the mattress, pulled the gun out, cocked it and pointed it at her husband. Shaking and scared, Clara looked at James and told him, "If you strike me again, I'll shoot." James looked awful, and something in his eyes this time truly scared Clara. He came at her again, and the last thing Clara remembered was the sound of the gun going off one time. After that, her mind went blank. She didn't remember shooting him two more times, only that she went outside and found James near death on the front porch steps.

James had staggered out of the apartment, trying to flee his wife, and collapsed on the porch. Mable Lytle, a neighbor, had wanted to borrow something from Clara and was privy to the start of everything. She had heard the glass breaking and seen the unknown man in the apartment looking rattled. Mable claimed she saw James attack Clara and knock her to the ground. Not wanting to be part of their argument, she rushed out of the apartment building and heard the sounds of gunfire behind her just as she got outside. Mabel picked up her pace as two more gunshots were heard. Once she got a distance away, she turned around in time to see James come out the front door, holding his hands over his bloody chest as he collapsed on the porch.

The next day, newspaper headlines read "Jealous Husband Killed by Wife." People thought that James had come home to find his wife with another man, but when the details of the trial started to spill out, they learned the truth was far from that.

Clara sat in jail for two months until November 19, 1907, when the trial started. She pleaded not guilty and claimed she had shot him in self-defense. On the witness stand, Clara was dressed in black with a veil over her face. Her adoptive mother sat next to her. As the lawyers began their questioning, she started to tell her life of "white slavery," as it was often referred to at the turn of the twentieth century. She told the horrible story of how her husband demanded she sell herself in order to bring in extra money, mostly to pay for his daily liquor expenses and disinclination to work. The *Grand Rapids Press* stated that the "testimony was unfit for publication" and used the headline "Story Is Revolting" in bold capital letters.

Since the start of their marriage, Clara and James had led a "nomadic life," going from city to city and finding jobs usually in hotel restaurants. The police were actually familiar with the two, and it was said they had been asked to leave Grand Rapids shortly before the shooting took place, although the exact reasons why are unknown. Altercations with the police in Muskegon and Jackson had also been reported and were tossed around as evidence by the prosecution, showing that Clara and James were nothing more than common lowlifes with no intent to be decent citizens.

Prosecutor McDonald dug up dirt on Clara's past and asked her about being arrested in Jackson for "parading the halls of her rooming house clad in men's clothing." He went on to suggest to the jury that Clara was the one who actually "wore the pants," as perhaps her men's clothing stint suggested, and that she was the one who was abusive toward James whenever she wasn't happy with him. He continued his argument by asking, "Is it not a fact, Mrs. Connolly, that you were able to thrash James whenever you so desired?"

"Well, I was able to defend myself," she retorted back.

"Now, isn't it a fact that in a fight you had with him at Muskegon you knocked him down and he received a broken arm?" the prosecutor asked.

"No, sir. He slipped down and broke his arm when we were quarreling," Clara responded.

The prosecutor's objective was to prove to the jury that Clara wasn't the innocent, victimized woman she claimed to be. He brought up her first marriage and said she had never led a "moral life" and that she had always been a "dissolute character and that her husband secured his divorce on statutory grounds." Reporters wrote, "She was no paragon of virtue."

Clara answered everything the prosecutor asked her with open honesty, but she stuck to her story. She said James convinced her that prostitution would be simple and easy money compared to working in hotels. Whatever her reasons were, she complied, and from that point on, James never worked again except for a few odd jobs. He essentially became his wife's pimp, running a one-girl bordello. James would sell beer to men who came to see her wherever they were staying and was even said to have rented a piano at one of the places they lived so he could entertain the men.

Clara's defense lawyer, attorney Ellis, argued that her early childhood spent in an orphan asylum was not the perfect start for a good upbringing. She had been forced to lead a life of "shameful degradation" and, in an attempt to protect herself, had used the gun on her husband out of desperation and fear of him. She was asked if she had intended to shoot him, and she said she had hoped the gun would just scare him. She never had any intention of killing him.

Ellis brought up James's character. How could someone ask his wife to sell herself to other men? What kind of man would do such a thing to someone he supposedly loved? It was clear to Ellis that the only thing on James's mind was money for himself and not the well-being of his wife.

In his closing statement, Prosecutor McDonald said, "She killed him, which you may say was a favor to society," but a killing was a killing, and punishment had to be dealt. On November 21, 1907, the jury returned a verdict of manslaughter. When the verdict was read, Clara cried loudly and fainted. The reporters for the *Grand Rapids Press* commented on the scene in the courtroom after the sentence was given:

> *For the moralist, the scene depicted a telling sermon upon the wages of sin. This woman, young, not long ago the wife of an honest man and the mother of two small children, separated from these through her own folly and then entering into a depraved and loathsome existence had met the inevitable end of the transgressor against the laws of God and man.*

Attorney Ellis was not happy with the outcome of the case and immediately asked for a new trial. He felt the prosecution purposely left out the most important witness in the case. That person was Frank Fisher, and he was the man who had been sent to the apartment that day by James. Ellis said the prosecution knew his testimony would weaken its case and he was never asked to testify. The judge gave Ellis three days to find Frank Fisher and get him to swear to the affidavit he had given Prosecutor McDonald, but Fisher was nowhere to be found.

On December 12, 1907, Clara was sentenced before Judge Stewart and was given two to fifteen years at the Detroit House of Correction for Women. The court felt a maximum of four years would be sufficient. A new trial was

Detroit House of Correction. *Courtesy of Library of Congress.*

also denied by the judge, as he hadn't seen anything unfair about the first trial. Clara listened to the sentence without a flicker of emotion on her face and asked that she be sent to the House of the Good Shepherd instead of Detroit, but the judge refused this. He gave Clara a final lecture and hoped that her time spent in jail would cause her to repent her old life and come out "upright" and a "better girl."

A SECOND CHANCE

Attorney Ellis never stopped fighting for Clara, and on July 6, 1909, a new trial for Clara was granted. The *Grand Rapids Press* reported the reason for the new trial and wrote, "The court holds it was an error to admit testimony relative to the defendant's chastity previous to her marriage to Sweeney." A few weeks later, on July 29, Clara was released, and it was decided to forgo another trial. Her first husband, George, the father of her two children, Ralph and Florence, came to pick her up. Clara was ready to go back to her former life. The *Grand Rapids Press* said, "She is a free woman and the period of this freedom depends upon herself. Indications point to a reunion of Hodgekinson and the woman who is the mother of his children, and this event it is believed will mark the final reformation of Clara Connolly."

Chapter 11

Who Killed Josephine Oom?

It was a very cold fall night on November 2, 1905. Josephine Oom, her older sister Jennie and their younger brother John were bundled up in their horse carriage heading to their home on East Bridge Street, now known as Michigan Street. The family lived on the outskirts of town, and as the buggy rode on, the street became darker and wooded. Just two days after Halloween, ghost stories were still fresh in the minds of everyone, and as the trio rode on into the woods, a hazy, luminescent white figure suddenly appeared on the road ahead of them.

Three pairs of eyes widened in curiosity as they tried to make out what the strange figure was. Was it a ghost? John clicked his tongue and urged the horse to go faster to try and catch up with the thing. But no matter how quickly they sped up, the figure stayed ahead of them and then suddenly vanished without a trace.

Everyone was completely befuddled, and as soon as they got home, they told everyone in the house what they had just witnessed. More excited than scared, they laughed it off, and it became known as "the ghost story" among the family. Little did they know that in just two weeks, the family would experience tragedy in the very spot where the ghostly apparition had disappeared.

On Wednesday, November 16, 1905, Josephine left work early, at 3:00 p.m., from her job as a stenographer for the Federal Audit Company. She headed to the home of her music teacher for a lesson and waited around for her brother John to pick up her and her older sister Jennie around 6:30 p.m.

Everyone was looking forward to being at home that night. The family had planned a party, and the girls had invited their friends John and Cornelius Vanderbout over to the house. John and Cornelius were brothers Josephine and Jennie had met when the two were visiting with family in Rochester, New York. The men were salesmen. They found themselves in Grand Rapids for a bit and looked up the girls, as they were the only people they knew in the city and had enjoyed their company back in Rochester.

As the horse buggy headed away from the city, the three chatted about their day and were suddenly startled by a voice and a man stepping out onto the road from the shadows of the woods. The man's voice yelled, "Throw up your hands!" but before anyone could react and do as told, the sounds of gunfire rang out in the crisp night. The horse reared up and panicked at the sound of the loud gunshots. John pulled the reins, managed to get the spooked animal under control and got the horse and carriage moving as fast as it would go, away from the area and the man who had just shot at them.

John was fine but rattled as he guided them home. Jennie's finger had been hit by one of the bullets and was throbbing with pain. Part of her finger bone was shattered. Josephine, on the other hand, was unresponsive and moved her head around just a little. She wasn't saying a word. Jennie knew Josephine had been shot, but in the dark, she had no idea where or how badly. John felt something warm running onto his hand after the bullets were fired, but he knew it wasn't from his body. As the horse pulled up to the home at top speed, John burst into the house and alerted the family as to what had just happened along the road. John and his father, Benjamin, carried Josephine out of the carriage and into the house. A doctor was sent for immediately, but there was nothing that could be done. The bullet had gone into her brain by her right temple. She had died almost immediately.

The shooting was tragic. The police suspected at first that the Ooms were being held up by an amateur highwayman who got nervous and botched the job by firing his gun off carelessly rather than using it to threaten the trio for whatever money or jewelry they had on them. The girls did not have boyfriends or any relationship problems that the police knew of, so the theory of a jealous lover was ruled out. John and Cornelius Vanderbout, who had planned on coming to the Oom house that night, were told right away about the shooting, and they got to the house quickly. The police jumped on the two men and started to question who they were and what their relationship to the two girls was. The brothers didn't appreciate getting pulled into a murder mystery but told the police that they were just friends of the girls and had no romantic interest in them.

The eldest Oom brother, William, told the police he had come home about twenty minutes before his siblings. Along the road, he saw a man darkly dressed standing alone along the road's edge. He had on a long coat and a hat and said nothing as William drove past him. Had this been the man who shot at the carriage? Was he waiting specifically for Josephine, Jennie and John? The whole thing was puzzling. Besides a random holdup, there didn't seem to be any obvious motive for the crime. Many men and even three boys were brought in for questioning, plus one hobo. None of them proved helpful in the mystery, and all were released.

Detectives Young, Viergever, McDonald and Sturgis were all assigned to the case, and the men jumped in headfirst and began interviewing as many people as possible who were connected to the Ooms. One of those people was Adrian Semeyn, who had been married to Jennie and Josephine's sister Lena, who had died at age twenty-eight in 1896, leaving Adrian a widower. Adrian continued to be part of the family, coming to the house at last once a week for dinner on Wednesday nights. Oddly enough, Adrian didn't come to the house that night per his usual schedule. He claimed the lousy, cold weather had kept him at home and he didn't want to venture outside.

Police learned that Adrian had started to show affection for Jennie shortly after his wife died, and this put him on the list of possible suspects. It was even said that when his wife had taken sick, Adrian had been seen walking Jennie home from dances in the evening. Police officers brought him down to the station and questioned him further but didn't gather much that would make them believe he had been the shooter.

Clues at the scene of the crime suggested the man wore pointed shoes, but not much else was learned. The police used a bloodhound in an effort to catch the scent of the stranger, but the dog wasn't able to latch onto anything. If they had brought the hound in as soon as the shooting had been reported, the dog might have been able to pick up the scent on the tree the man had been standing behind before he stepped out into the road and aimed his gun.

Josephine's funeral was held the day after she died at the family's home. A church service followed at Trinity Lutheran Church. Their home could barely contain the number of friends, family and well-wishers who came to say their last goodbyes to Josephine. One tearful friend told the crowd in the home that when Josephine walked down the street, every dog would run up to her with their tails wagging in the hopes of getting their heads patted. Children absolutely adored her, and kids who had only said "hello" to her on the streets as she passed came to take a last look at her pretty face. She was simply loved by everyone, which made the whole thing that much harder to digest. There was just no rhyme or reason for what had happened. The *Grand Rapids Press* wrote, "After forty eight hours the murder of Josephine Oom seems to have settled back in the basis of an unfathomable mystery, whose every detail apparently leads the authorities only deeper in the maze of uncertainty." She was laid to rest in Oak Hills Cemetery.

Theories were getting desperate; one of the most pathetic ideas was that maybe a woman had committed the crime. The *Grand Rapids Press* suggested that if a woman had been the criminal, that was why the job was "botched," and said, "The theory may not be worth anything but at any rate, the job was a nervous, bungling affair, just about what you would expect of a woman."

News of the shooting had spread throughout the state. The *Flint Journal* suggested the shooting was the byproduct of "bad literature"; someone had been trying to act out what they had read in a crime novel. The paper wrote, "Trashy literature is one of the most serious problems of the present time and one of the most difficult with which to deal." Over a century ago, people blamed the media for the problems in the world, just like many do today.

By November 20, the detectives hadn't put anyone behind bars yet. Residents of Grand Rapids didn't like the fact that there could be a gun-toting lunatic lurking in the dark, waiting to jump out at another family going home at night. People living in Grand Rapids' east side were scared. Many people who hadn't even considered it before purchased guns. Women were not opening their doors to anyone once the sun set. Everyone's feeling of security had been shaken. Regular citizens pooled their money together to generate a decent reward to be offered to anyone who could provide information regarding the mystery. By November 22, the cash reward was up to $950, a substantial amount for 1905.

As the weeks went on, the reward money was unclaimed and the detectives hadn't succeeded in attaining one useful clue. To the police, that meant either that whoever had done the crime was a complete stranger to the city and left as soon as he fired the fatal shots or that the person who killed Josephine Oom and injured Jennie was the only person who knew what had happened, and that person wasn't going to talk for anything.

Six weeks after Josephine's death, the coroner finally went forward with the inquest on December 27 to determine the official cause of death. That's when things started to get exciting again, as some rather shocking details that were neglected to be told at the start came out. Eighteen-year-old John Oom was the first to take the witness stand. All he could do was retell the story of what had happened while he was steering their carriage that night with his two sisters. His story was the same as the first time he told it, fresh after it had happened. Coroner Hilliker described the bullet found in Josephine's head.

Then Jennie sat down on the witness stand and completely turned the case upside down. She had been hiding the fact that she and Adrian had been dating. Jennie confessed she had actually been engaged to Adrian Semeyn, her former brother-in-law, for two years but had called it off back in August. She still continued to talk to him, but he didn't seem to understand that she didn't want to marry him anymore. He would wait for her outside her work.

Myrtle Emmons, a co-worker of Jennie's, testified that she had seen Adrian waiting across the street for Jennie the night before the shooting and had seen him other nights in the past. The night before the murder, Adrian seemed very agitated that Jennie was outside talking to a man and woman. Myrtle said she saw Adrian across the street, pacing back and forth and glaring at Jennie.

Kittie Huffman worked with Jennie and said she had seen Adrian and Jennie at the skating rink at Reed's Lake the weekend before the murder. Jennie introduced Kittie to Adrian, and Kittie remembered Jennie telling him she wasn't any good at skating. Adrian remarked that they could come back on Monday and he would teach her how to skate, as he was quite good at it. Jennie ended up not showing up to Reed's Lake in favor of going out with her sister and the two brothers from New York. Belle Beach, Jennie's manager at the store, had noticed she was getting attention from three different men at that time and warned her, "You better look out, or someone will be getting jealous."

Jennie's mother, Maggie, told her she didn't want Adrian around the house anymore. This upset Jennie, so she told her mother that if he couldn't come around the house, then it was time she leave it. Maggie testified that she wasn't opposed to Adrian as a husband, but the fact that he had been married to her oldest daughter bothered her, and she didn't see the marriage as appropriate. She also mentioned that Adrian had been in some "trouble" in the past and had left the state for a brief period.

An aunt of Jennie's got on the witness stand and said she had never liked Adrian paying attention to her niece and she let her opinion be known to Jennie's mother. There had been rumors about Jennie and Adrian while her sister was sick and dying. It was very suspicious to Prosecutor Brown that the family had been extremely quiet in regard to the relationship status between their son-in-law and daughter and that Jennie hadn't mentioned any of this when originally questioned about him by the police.

The original city hall, where many of the coroner's inquests took place. *Courtesy of Library of Congress.*

When William Oom, the eldest brother, was called to testify, he told how he had come through the area just twenty minutes before the rest of his family and had seen a strange man wearing a dark hat and long coat. William felt that the man he had seen that night was much smaller than Adrian in height and weight. William stated that Josie had had dates here and there, but he wasn't aware that Jennie had "steady company." He had no clue that Adrian had proposed to his sister and that the two had been seeing each other for two years.

Adrian had come to the attention of the police more than once since Josephine's death, but the family had full faith that he had nothing to do with the crime. The confession of Jennie's past engagement injected the story with the "jealous lover" scenario, and judging by Jennie's and other witnesses' stories, it certainly seemed as if Adrian was indeed the jealous type. As the inquest carried on through the weeks, the courtroom was packed with the curious public hanging on to every word confessed and hoping to be present when the whole story was exposed.

The holidays ended, and a new year moved in. The inquest continued onward and even went into a panic on January 17, 1906. The photographers were told they could not take pictures during the inquest, but Cecil Lane, excited to capture the moment, fired his camera with a new type of flash that made everyone think a gun had just gone off. Jennie reacted quickly to the flash powder and put her head down on the witness stand. When people looked around after the flash and loud sound, they thought the shooter had come back to finish his work and Jennie had been shot, as her head was down. The crowded courtroom panicked, and everyone headed for the doors. The judge banged his gavel loudly and got the room to calm down, returning everything to order again. The photographer was promptly arrested for contempt.

Finally, after a whole year had passed, Adrian was put on the stand to testify. Why it had taken so long was anyone's guess. Adrian spoke slowly and was described as "sullen." He said he had gone with Jennie for two to three years. He refused to answer whether he had been engaged to her and became a little cocky when asked those questions, feeling they were personal and only his business. He claimed they called off their relationship because she "didn't like the other women he was keeping company with." He further claimed he had no idea who would have wanted to shoot the two women and felt it was a rogue highwayman. The prosecutor asked his questions but couldn't trip Adrian up on anything. It was all still a mystery and, it seemed, would forever remain that way. The coroner's jury concluded that "Josephine Oom came to her death from a gunshot wound inflicted by some person unknown."

The Case Is Resurrected

Four years later, in October 1909, Josephine's murder once again appeared in the headlines. Sheriff Hurley took an active interest in reviving the Oom murder case after getting a few new tips he wanted to follow up on. Peter Overbock, an inmate at the Asylum for the Criminally Insane in Ionia, had started to talk about the Oom murder, saying his old partner in crime, William Stegenga, had been the one who killed the girl, having made plans to hold up their carriage.

Stegenga had actually been one of the men questioned shortly after Josephine was shot. Detectives Youngs and Viergever knew the man had a bad reputation and had been in and out of prison his whole life. William had just been shot by a police officer after attempting to rob a grocery store around the end of November 1905 and was in the hospital recovering when the two detectives came in, asking him about crimes that had been committed in the city, especially the Oom murder. If he didn't do it, maybe his companions in the underworld of Grand Rapids had said something to him, but he maintained he didn't know a thing about the case.

Prosecutor Brown paid a visit to the asylum and interviewed Peter about his time with William. Along with Peter's admittance of William being the shooter, Brown learned about many petty crimes William had gotten away with over the years. When Sheriff Hurley had to bring a prisoner up to Marquette, Prosecutor Brown rode with him so they could interview William Stegenga, who was doing fifteen years for burglary.

Prosecutor Brown was granted an interview with Stegenga and started to question him about his petty crimes. William reluctantly admitted to the crimes told by Peter, and that's when Brown suddenly dropped the question, "Did you murder Josie Oom?" William quickly flared up and got defensive. He learned that his old pal Peter was the one accusing him of the Oom murder. William stated that Peter was clearly crazy, as he was locked up at the asylum, and it wasn't right that the sheriff and prosecutor were just taking him on his word. Sheriff Hurley said, "I am as sure Stegenga is the man who did the job as that I am sitting here. We are on the right track." The next step was to get him released from Marquette and officially charge him with the murder so a trial could be set up. They had hoped the man would just break down and confess.

William wrote an intelligent and well-written letter to the *Evening Press*, basically saying he didn't kill Josephine and that the prosecutor and sheriff were trying to pin the murder on him with nothing but circumstantial evidence so they could put an unsolved murder to bed. He wrote that the men were trying to force him into a confession based on his past criminal behavior and the words of a crazy man in an asylum. William was only serving a potential three- to fifteen-year sentence for burglary, but if he were to be wrongly accused of murder, he would never get out of prison. Sheriff Hurley worked this angle of the case for a year, but nothing came of it.

Does it seem possible that a jealous Adrian could have fired the shots, upset and angry at Jennie, who had upset him by breaking off the rather secret engagement and then snubbing him at the skating rink? There were enough eyewitnesses who reported on Adrian's behavior toward Jennie before the murder happened. Or was the man who killed Josie Oom just a random person who panicked during an unfortunate holdup and shot the girl, never intending to kill anyone? The truth is probably lost in time now, but the story goes down in history as one of the unsolved murders in the history of Grand Rapids.

Chapter 12

The Scarlet Sisterhood
of Grand Rapids

T hey had that in Grand Rapids?" was the comment I usually got with a raised eyebrow when talking about my research into nineteenth- and early twentieth-century houses of prostitution. While we may think of bigger cities like Chicago, New York or Detroit as having red-light districts, Grand Rapids was in no short supply of painted ladies and bold madams who only add to its colorful, "wicked" past. Not much is known about some of them, as their tales were only preserved in snippets of police blotter in the newspapers, but through those preserved gems, just enough is there to learn about what they were like while alive. Their lives were wild ones, and most prostitutes and madams lived fast and hard. My goal was to bring to the surface some of these long-forgotten women and stories from bawdier times in Grand Rapids.

THE BUSINESS OF "FALLEN WOMEN"

There was no shortage of job titles for prostitutes; painted ladies, women of easy virtue, sporting ladies, frail ones, ladies of the evening, working girls, nymph du pave, streetwalkers, scarlet sisters, the demimonde and soiled doves are just a handful of them. Houses of prostitution also had their many names: brothels, bawdyhouses, disorderly houses and houses of ill repute, to name a few. Women who got involved in the business did not typically do so because they wanted to. It was usually because they had no other choice in life.

All too often, the women came from broken homes, having parents who kicked them out at a young age to fend for themselves. Some were widows with children to support or, worse, had been abandoned by their husbands, leaving them destitute. Many had acquired drug habits that needed quick money to appease. Prostitutes hooked on opium, morphine and alcohol were found in record numbers working in houses of ill repute, as they were commonly called in Grand Rapids. Lack of education and mental health were also blamed for women going into the flesh business.

Jobs common to women in the nineteenth century might pay under ten dollars a week, which would barely cover rent and hungry mouths to feed. If a woman turned to prostitution, she could bring in twenty to more than one hundred dollars a week if she were in high demand. It's no wonder why women pushed their morals aside and signed up to be part of the "scarlet sisterhood." The money was extremely tempting if one could overlook the negative consequences that came with the territory.

Women were often tricked into the business by a "procuress," a prostitute who sought to ensnare other women into a "life of shame." It was her job to hustle up new women to work at a brothel. Many young girls looking for normal work got involved in prostitution by believing that the procuress was offering them honest work somewhere. Old job advertisements in newspapers would even trick women into believing they were applying for honest work. The ad might be requesting a cook, housekeeper or seamstress. The woman would go to the address given only to learn about the "character" of the place after it was too late. Entrapment like this started to happen more and more and was commonly referred to as "white slavery," as the girls would be threatened to do things they did not want or ever intend to do.

In December 1892, Maggie Cook, a procuress working for a brothel in northern Michigan, came to Grand Rapids and Ionia in search of lost girls to bring back with her. She succeeded in procuring two girls from Ionia, and on her next stop in Grand Rapids, she left them at one of the bawdyhouses in town while she went out in search of more girls. She was described as a "hideous appearing wretch, bearing the semblance of a woman." The madam of the house the girls were left at liked the look of them and saw them as "keepers" for her own house. When she learned Maggie had just temporarily placed them there with the intention of bringing them up north with her, the madam of the house was annoyed and promptly told a detective what Maggie was up to. When the police showed up at the train depot to confront Maggie and the two girls before they left town, they had their stories prepared. The girls said they were good friends and were going up to visit one of their aunts in a northern town. Maggie told the police they were traveling to the same place, and as she was worried about them, she wanted to look after the young girls to see that they were kept safe while traveling. When they were questioned separately, the girls broke down and told the officers their real plans. Maggie was arrested.

A very small percentage of women entered the "dark side" because there was something alluring about it. If a girl could get into one of the high-end parlors, she could make excellent money, have a nice room to stay in and wear beautiful dresses. For a few young, pretty women, the lifestyle seemed like a good career. Some hoped for the romanticized idea that they would become "kept women" and wealthy, handsome men desiring mistresses would take care of them and lavish them with gifts and other fine things. This, of course, was very rare.

A DANGEROUS PROFESSION

The risks of a prostitute in the nineteenth century were innumerable. Disease, early death, suicide, unwanted pregnancy, drug addiction and being beaten or raped were all very real factors a woman had to contend with. Even the madam of the house was known to throw in a punch or two if she felt one of her girls deserved it. Syphilis and gonorrhea were common maladies that could slowly waste a person away over years. Gonorrhea was the lesser evil of the two and could sometimes leave a woman sterile, which was what a lot of women in the business hoped to become. It was commonly thought that prostitutes contracted disease because they were not "pure." The men were never blamed for being part of the problem and spreading disease.

Pregnancy was a scary ordeal, especially in the 1800s. Not only was the birthing process dangerous, but if prostitution was a woman's chosen career and she didn't plan on changing that, a pregnancy could severely impact the amount of money she was able to make for many months. Abortions were illegal and dangerous, and if a woman could find someone to perform one, the chances of infection or a botched job could lead to death, as many of the places where they were done were not a typical sterile hospital setting.

Corrupt doctors could work for a house of prostitution and give the women fake certificates of health. Men were aware of the health dangers when buying time with a prostitute. Venereal disease ran rampant in many of these places. It was the job of the madam to make sure men felt safe and at ease with her girls. Working girls would often have a certificate of health that would have been signed by a doctor to prove to a man that they were disease free. In some cases, a man would get a disease from a lady who had claimed to be free of any issues. The doctor who gave her the fake medical certificate would then be referred to the man, who now needed to pay a doctor to be treated for what he had picked up from the woman. The whole thing was a vicious circle.

Perhaps the worst repercussion of the job and the hardest to recover from was becoming a complete outcast from society. Prostitutes were considered to be at the bottom of the totem pole, the lowest of the low; it was known as the "unforgivable sin." Once a woman went down that path, she was marked and not often let back into polite society. Even the most charitable, "Christian" person all too often looked away from a prostitute trying to better herself or reaching out for help. So heavy was their reputation that people just looked at them like they didn't exist. The *Grand Rapids Evening Leader* from September 10, 1887, wrote, "Gentle ladies, who will go to the gutters to rescue men from their degradation or to distant lands to save the heathen, will draw their skirts and avert their eyes at the approach of a Magdalene. Even in the sanctuary the woman who has sinned is not welcomed, and a sneer would be her worldly share should she fall on her knees in prayer." The article went on to say, "This city has its full quota of wicked women, and they are of every degree and condition, those who fell through faith in false promises, and those whom starvation drove to shame, and those whose vicious inclinations lead them easily and naturally to the gilded mansions of sin."

PROSTITUTION AND THE LAW

Jail time and fines were common if a woman was caught plying her trade. Prostitution was technically illegal, but the police often looked the other way and let it exist, usually with the help of bribes and favors. If caught, the women would have to appear in court and be fined or serve jail time if they didn't have the money, as it was considered a misdemeanor. The revenue from the fines collected from disorderly houses and individual women was quite the sum, and the early papers of Grand Rapids are riddled with women having to pay up for their "dishonest work." Their names would appear in the papers but never the men who were paying for their services.

Fines from prostitution were considerable and went toward funding public institutions around Grand Rapids. On the night of July 19, 1874, Police Chief Moran felt it was high time for a good raid, seeing as many of Chicago's "fallen ones" had recently fled that city and come to Michigan to continue to find work. Raids were common, and when the police decided to do one, they would pick a house—maybe one that wasn't in good standing—and arrest the women and men who were found inside. Property owners and madams who got in good with the police received fewer raids of their places. All in all, the night's raid put forty-two people behind bars. The higher-class girls in their beautiful dresses just paid their fines at the jail and didn't have to appear in court the next morning for sentencing. The less fortunate had to appear in court. The *Grand Rapids Daily Democrat* wrote, "As a result of the raid we never saw a more dejected looking lot of men, or a more indifferent set of women, nor heard a great assortment of lame excuses, than were offered in examination of their offenses." The amount of $541.87 was collected after everyone emptied their wallets. The money went to the public library.

In March 1886, Michigan changed its laws and made running a house of ill repute a felony. The new law, act No. 34, public acts of 1887, stated:

> *Every person who shall keep a house of ill-fame, resorted to for the purpose of prostitution or lewdness, and every person who shall solicit, or in any manner induce a female to enter such house for the purpose of becoming a prostitute, or shall by force, fraud, deceit, or in any like manner procure a female to enter such house for the purpose of prostitution or of becoming a prostitute, shall be deemed guilty of a felony and upon conviction thereof shall be punished by imprisonment in the state prison not more than five years, or in the county jail not more than one year, or by fine not exceeding one thousand dollars or by both such fine and imprisonment, in the discretion of the court.*

Grand Rapids had its own set of local laws that prohibited prostitution and houses of ill fame that had been passed by the Common Council of the City of Grand Rapids in July 1875. The laws stated that anyone who owned a house could not lease it out as a brothel. Maintaining a house of ill repute or aiding one was illegal. It was also illegal to set foot in a brothel, so the patrons could get fined as well. Last, the police did not need a search warrant to invade a suspected house at any time of the day or night if they thought prostitution was going on inside.

While the laws prohibited people from renting their property for the purpose of prostitution, it didn't stop property owners from doing it. Many houses had what was called a silent partner. This was usually the owner of the house who very well knew that a madam had set her ladies up in his property. Many prominent men in politics and business in Grand Rapids had secret stakes in houses of prostitution. They could purchase cheap property and charge high rent. If a house was owned by someone high enough on the social ladder, the house could be "overlooked" by police and raids kept to a minimum.

The *Telegram Herald* pointed out that a house on Kent Street was owned by Joseph A. Martin, who was a "capitalist and prominent church leader," and another house on the same street was owned by the E.P. Fuller estate, whose family had many "prominent Sunday school workers." These men knew what their rented properties were being used for, and during a time when newspapers actually had some power, the *Telegram Herald* hoped that publishing the property owners' names would cause them to do something about the "blight" they were allowing to happen close to the heart of the city.

PARLOR GIRLS TO STREETWALKERS

Like all businesses out there, quality varied. Houses of prostitution differed from the low-end hovels to the high-end parlor houses that catered to the wealthy and elite. Many houses had a covered, private side entrance where men could enter discreetly and not have to stand at a front door ringing a doorbell for all to see on the street. Brothels were not typically marked, but anyone looking for one could talk to the right person and be pointed in the right direction.

At a higher-end parlor house, good food and expensive wine would be served. If men got too drunk and rude, they would be asked to leave. Men were expected to be clean and respectful. The price of alcohol was tripled at these places, allowing for huge profit. Only the rich men could usually afford to patronize places of this caliber, as sometimes a one-night stay with a woman could run upward of $250, which was a lot of money in the 19th century. Women in the high-end places were not allowed to drink on the job and needed to keep their wits and manners together. The women working in these houses were young and beautiful.

Women who worked in the high-end houses were often in debt to the madam of the house. The ladies were expected to have very fine dresses of expensive material, and if a woman came in new to the job without these things, the madam would pay for the dresses. This meant that the girl not only had to work for her rent and food but also had to pay off her pricy attire and many times stay in debt, as the quick and abundant cash caused a lot of women to live fast and spend their money carelessly. Being in debt to the madam sometimes made it hard for the girl to move on or change houses if she wanted to.

As glamorously as some girls lived, their lives were not usually ones of joy and happiness. They were still filled with sorrow and the knowledge that they were not considered to be part of polite society and never would be unless they left the area and started over somewhere else far away.

Women were typically allowed to keep half of their earnings, but the rest went to the house. Some of the young, pretty girls became somewhat wealthy very fast, but if they didn't save any of their money, they became destitute, as prostitutes peaked at a young age. Men wanted pretty and youthful girls, and as soon as a wrinkle or a gray hair showed, a woman's career in the high-end house was over, and it was a downward spiral from there. The next place to go was known as a common brothel.

Women in the common brothels were not always pretty or young, and the prices were much cheaper. These places were more like a bar setting, where drinks were served and music was played. They could be found above saloons or in the back of dance halls. Police raids happened more often at these joints.

Sidney Smith owned a two-story building on West Bridge Street in March 1880. His saloon was downstairs, but the upstairs was rented out to women. Sidney was busted and had to pay a fifty-dollar fine or serve six months at the prison in Ionia. The judge lectured him on his bad business dealings and stated, "At least three fourths of the crime committed in Grand Rapids primarily originated in three combined saloons and houses of ill fame. He could not conceive of anything so degrading in its character as for a man to engage in such business, and no one with a spark of manhood or principle about him would be found in such dealings."

Low-end brothels were just what the title evoked. These prostitutes were not your supermodels of the day. Many of them suffered from drug addiction. Protection of the women from a bouncer wasn't always available. It could be quite common to catch venereal diseases at these places. Men were not expected to be gentlemen and could come into the house filthy from a hard day's work and not be expected to clean up—just pay up.

The bottom of the food chain and most dangerous position in prostitution was the lonely streetwalker, who didn't have a house to work at and tried to solicit any male off the street. Streetwalkers had to be kept away from the houses so as not to take away any of their business for cheap. These ladies didn't have the protection of a bouncer like in a house and could easily end up beaten and left to die. Some of these women had severe drug problems, and not even a low-end place would accept their behavior.

Kent Street, which is now Bond Avenue Northeast, was well known for its streetwalkers at one time. The *Grand Rapids Democrat* reported that people were complaining about the women of the street, saying their "sense of decency has been shocked by the brazen overtures of these creatures." The police went undercover in plain clothes and walked down the street. A couple women finally came up to them and made suggestions, and they were promptly arrested for "disorderly conduct." Six women were arrested during their one-night undercover sting.

THE MADAM

The madam, or "proprietress," as Grand Rapids papers called her, was essentially the boss. Author Michael Rutter in his book *Upstairs Girls* wrote, "A madam was a feudal lord in her own fiefdom." Her word was law, and if you didn't like it, you didn't have a job. He also wrote, "In a good house, a madam had to be a good businesswoman, a psychologist, a mother, and a disciplinarian. She also needed to know what political wheels to grease. The madam was responsible for paying the boarders, the rent, the bartender, the piano player, the bouncer, taking care of the licenses, fees, fines and bribes and keeping the bar stocked." If a house didn't have a good madam, it wasn't a well-run business.

Many madams were like mothers to their girls and were loved by everyone, but some of the madams were known to be mean, greedy and vicious women for whom no girl wanted to work. Susie Cane died in Grand Rapids on March 23, 1893, and was considered the "Empress of Old Almy" street and the "Queen of the Resorts on Waterloo." Susie's small obituary read, "She died unwept, unhonored and unsung. She died an outcast and even the creatures whom she once reigned over looked upon her with loathing and disgust." If you died an outcast among the outcasts, you must have been an awful person.

The Scarlet Sisters of Grand Rapids

The notorious parts of Grand Rapids during the mid-nineteenth and early twentieth centuries were streets known then as Almy, Canal and Kent. Almy was removed in 1905 and was around the vicinity of where Van Andel Arena is presently. Kent is now Bond Avenue NW, and Canal is now Monroe Street. Many other brothels existed on other streets, but these were the most talked-about areas in the old newspapers. The women who lived this lifestyle were interesting characters, and much of their history was never recorded and has been forgotten. These women were not the "victors" in society, so their stories were never written. Rutter said it best in his study of old prostitution: "Their stories are loud, ribald, bold and sassy, tragic and pitiful, but important and worth telling." The same goes for the ladies of Grand Rapids' past "sisterhood." While considered outcasts, they are still part of the city's extensive history.

Around the area of Louis Street, one of the rougher-looking parts of town that not everyone wanted to walk through. *Courtesy of the Grand Rapids Public Library.*

A photo showing the "seedier" parts of town or "Shantytown" around Louis Street. *Courtesy of the Grand Rapids Public Library.*

Area around Fuller and Louis Streets. Not many pictures exist of the "shadier areas" of town, but these gems offer a glimpse. *Courtesy of the Grand Rapids Public Library.*

Georgie Young, Grand Rapids' Most Famous Madam

Georgie Young earned notoriety in Grand Rapids during the decade from 1879 to 1889. She gained prominence by running one of the most famous brothels in Grand Rapids on the infamous Almy Street. She grew up very poor and, by thirty-one years of age, was a powerful businesswoman in the underworld. She owned her own property, and it was said that she made several hundred dollars a week, which would equal about $16,000 by today's standards.

In 1889, she decided to "repent" her old ways and turn a new leaf, leaving the prostitution business behind. The Moral Purity Movement was in full swing at the time, and women who worked in prostitution, especially the ladies who ran establishments, were urged to quit and seek salvation from God.

Georgie's Downfall

Georgie was born in 1858 in South Creek, Pennsylvania, as Jennie Wetmore. It was common for women in prostitution not to use their real names to protect their families. Her father died when she was only six months old, and her mother, Harriet, was left financially struggling to care for six children all under ten years of age. Georgie and her twin brother, Jared, were the youngest. The 1860 census of South Creek shows their real estate value at only $250 and personal estate at $20. They were the poorest family on the census record among their fellow neighbors.

The family eventually left Pennsylvania and moved to Illinois to be closer to Harriet's father, and as the children got older, they left to work for their food and board and lighten the burden on their mother. Harriet's eldest son, William, eventually moved to Sand Lake, Michigan, and made his home on the land their father had purchased there when he was still alive. In 1872, Georgie and her mother moved to Sand Lake, but they never felt welcome and were treated as more of an annoyance by William.

In September 1872, fifteen-year-old Georgie went to the fair in Grand Rapids with her older brother Melvin, and that's when her entire life changed overnight. She became separated from him, and as night descended on Grand Rapids, Georgie, crying, was approached by a woman named Jennie Holden. Jennie asked Georgie what was wrong, and she explained to the stranger that she had lost her brother and had no idea where she was, as this was the first time she had ever been to Grand Rapids. Jennie invited her to come back to her house for the night and told her they would go back to the fair the next morning and look for her brother.

When daylight broke, they went back to the fair, but Melvin was nowhere to be found. Jennie had invited her friend Charlie Young to go with them, a young man who had nothing going for him and was already well known to the police, but Georgie didn't know that. Georgie told her life story to Charlie, and he told the young girl that he owned a house and if they married, she could invite her mother to come live with them. Georgie was completely ignorant to the ways of the world, and only wanting to help her struggling mother and feeling desperate, she agreed to go with Jennie and Charlie to the judge's house, say she was seventeen when asked her age and marry Charlie Young. It didn't feel right to her, but she thought that perhaps God had brought Charlie to her to help her family's situation.

From that point on, her life became one trial after another. Charlie, of course, had lied to her. It's not known if he, with the help of Jennie, wanted to use her for prostitution, as Jennie already dabbled freely in the business. Charlie skipped town to Canada after the papers heard he had married a "fifteen"-year-old girl. Charlie's mother was especially upset that she now had to care for the girl after her son left. She was a stern, mean woman and blamed Georgie for what her son had done, saying it was her fault because she had lied to the judge to ensnare her son and get him in trouble.

Georgie was hurt and confused because the whole time she had only wanted to help her mother. Harriet had been deeply religious, always telling her daughter that "God would provide for the fatherless." After Georgie had spoken to police about her situation as a "lost girl," they sent a message to her brother in Sand Lake, but no response ever came back. He truly did not want to take care of his young sister and didn't care that she sat abandoned in Grand Rapids. It's not known if he ever told their mother she had written, but at some point, her mother did learn of her marriage and was rather shocked but figured that God had a plan.

Charlie's mom tossed Georgie out of the house and told her to go look for work. She didn't have references, so no one was interested in taking her on as a worker. Georgie walked the streets of Grand Rapids and knocked on the doors of homes. Knocking on the door of a particularly nice home, Georgie was greeted by a woman and asked her if she needed a girl to help with anything. The woman had in fact asked for help recently and asked Georgie if she could take care of children. She said she could, but when she was asked for her references, Georgie couldn't supply any and didn't even

Old Canal Street, where Georgie started at Mate Elliot's high-end parlor. *Courtesy of Library of Congress.*

An antique postcard of Canal Street, 1913. *Author's collection.*

know what that meant. She told the woman the truth about who she was, as it had been in the papers, and the woman coldly told her she wasn't wanted there and closed the door in her face.

Georgie never forgot that day. She felt like lying about her age got her in all this trouble, and when she told the truth to someone, that didn't seem to make a difference either. Her faith had been shaken. Georgie wrote in her autobiography, "Do you think in that last day, God will ask for references of some poor girl whose only sin is poverty?" Not wanting to go back to the mother of Charlie Young, she went to the only place she knew: Jennie Holden's house.

Jennie said she was leaving town and would take Georgie with her and help her find a job. From that point on, Georgie spent time in Jackson, Indiana and Kalamazoo brothels, not even knowing what was going on at first. The women smoked, drank and swore, things she was not used to. They seemed "different" and were nothing like her mother. She was ignorant of what was going on because she had never been taught prostitution existed.

Jackson police were alerted that two "old cats" were in town when Georgie showed up with Jennie. When Georgie heard this, she actually asked Jennie what they meant because they didn't own any cats. Jennie just laughed at her. She thought her ignorance was funny. Within the year, Georgie found herself in and out of jail and the workhouse. She finally ended up with her first "reference" from a Detroit man who sent Georgie to Mate Elliot's high-end place at 300 Canal Street in Grand Rapids. She was loaned nice clothes and started to accept her place working in the underworld. She eventually wrote to her mother, whom she found out was living in Grand Haven with a sister. She never told her what she had been through and certainly didn't let her know what line of work she had fallen into.

Georgie worked her way up the corporate ladder and by her early twenties, found herself quite the proprietress and the owner of much real estate in the city. By 1879, Georgie was the madam of a house on Almy Street, and occasionally her girls and men were making news in the papers. In December 1880, two of her girls were arrested; one of them was only fifteen. In 1881, her place was raided and five women and four male prostitutes were fined. In July of the same year, she was fined for selling alcohol without a city license and paid a fine of $28.57. She paid up and went right back to her work.

Clearing the "Dives"

By 1887, at the age of twenty-nine, Georgie owned entire city blocks. The police started to investigate the blocks owned for "immoral purposes." Names listed in the *Grand Rapids Evening Leader* were Delos A. Blodgett, Georgie Young, Jennie Harris, Mate Morrison, Agnes Carpenter, Minnie Brown, Nellie Hedges, Nellie Smith and Cora Ford. Discussions were had about how to control these areas. Alderman DeGraaf admitted that some of the keepers stayed good with the law by reporting who their girls were and running classier establishments. The alderman stated that "he was in favor of giving some protection to the law-abiding portion of the demimonde." They had come to the conclusion it was better to work with the social evil and cooperate with the women who were willing to keep orderly houses. Often, the soiled doves helped police and could be asked about scoundrels they were looking for. The women knew a lot about the criminals and perpetrators who lurked around the seedy parts of the city, and if they told their secrets, it could give them a "pass" the next time they were busted. The *Grand Rapids Evening Leader* wrote, "These women have more secrets than even the police."

The year 1887 was a bad time to be a prostitute or proprietress, as Superintendent Israel Smith was on a mission to rid the city of vice. On June 27, 1887, he decided to battle Kent Street for some of the heavy hitters in the business who owned quite an amount of property on the street. The Kent Street houses had typically been left alone in the past, as the owners were smart about their business and didn't do things to aggravate the police. Many of the homes did not have permanent boarders in them, so the girls didn't actually live there. It was just the place used when the men called for a lady. Some of the houses on Kent Street had private entrances so the public wouldn't know who was going into the place. Secrecy was very important, especially for the "gentlemen" and more prominent citizens who succumbed to the vice every once in a while.

But the Kent Street houses were too close to the booming business district in Grand Rapids, and Superintendent Smith wanted them cleared or moved. The police didn't want to make a big scene, so they went undercover down Kent Street on a Saturday afternoon, when the number of people visiting the homes would be low.

Through their investigation, they arrested "Madame Sarah Glover of 35 Kent. Mrs. Annie Rose of 40 Kent, Lou Morrison of 58 Kent and Fanny Withey at 60 Kent." All the women except Fanny, who claimed she

The original courthouse building. *Courtesy of Library of Congress.*

was sick, showed up to their court date the next morning. They pleaded not guilty and demanded a trial. Normally, these women would just pay their fines and leave, so the not guilty plea shocked Superintendent Smith. He made plans to gather many witnesses who had been seen going into their houses.

In 1887, it was getting harder and harder to run a good house. Prostitution was now a federal offense, and many of the long-standing houses were closing their doors. Jennie Turner, who owned a place on Almy, closed her place and moved to the east side of the state to start over. Nellie Gordon, once considered "the most beautiful woman in the city" and a courtesan, had retired and was living an honorable life. And the powerful Georgie Young decided to throw in the towel as well. The gilded age of Grand Rapids' houses of prostitution was coming to a close. Through women's reform groups, Georgie and other women were led to believe that they could repent for their past sins, turn their lives around for the better and encourage others to follow suit.

The Emerson Home for Fallen Women

To really prove she had changed for the better, Georgie had her huge house on Almy Street, sometimes called "The Castle," moved to a different location. In *The History of the City of Grand Rapids*, it was said that she "put about $8,000 of 'wages of iniquity' to a Christian use" to remodel and turn it into the Emerson Home for Fallen Women. The home would offer a refuge to women who wanted to get out of prostitution and make better lives for themselves. In an effort to spread the word about women's reform, Georgie wrote an autobiography in 1889 called *A Magdalen's Life*, explaining how she got into the business. She always felt that if someone had been there to help her in the beginning, her life would never have gone the way it did. One thousand copies were printed, and all the proceeds went to support the Emerson Home. The book sold fast. Citizens were hoping for a juicy tell-all about the life of a well-known prostitute and proprietress, but the book was the complete opposite of that. Georgie even said she didn't want to write something sensational. Her goal was to "arouse in people who have no feeling but condemnation for these women—a desire to aid in lifting them."

The Emerson Home was one of the first of its kind in Grand Rapids and catered to the women whom much of society had ignored for decades and considered less than human. Women were finally given a chance at real help and, best of all, hope.

Citizens of Georgie's day speculated if her transformation into a repentant woman was sincere. She was a powerful woman during her reign and built up a successful business and a good relationship with the police. By today's standards, she had turned herself into a millionaire. It was decided by the board of trustees of the Emerson Home that Georgie should take the wheel and be the matron of the house for a bit. She knew the business, and it was felt that she would be the best at convincing girls to turn away from the dangerous lifestyle. People kept a close eye on the house, wondering if Georgie wasn't just operating her brothel under the guise of the new "Christian" image. Superintendent Smith was especially suspicious while Georgie was in charge.

Jenny Percy, a girl who had gone to the house for help, told Superintendent Smith that she saw Georgie and her assistant "entertain male company… playing cards, smoking and drinking." This behavior certainly wasn't in line with the character of the place, and Smith alerted the board that he suspected Georgie was back to her old ways at the Emerson. Georgie was livid. Smith was a constant thorn in her side, even after she reformed. The whole thing ended up being a blow-up from rumors and lies, and the board still stuck to their belief that Georgie was a good fit as the matron. In an article from the *Daily Eagle*, members of the board wrote, "Supt. Smith admitted that his [Smith's] object was not to prove the impurity of Miss Young, but to show that a Christian woman, in whom the public would have confidence, should be placed at the head of the institution as matron." The board agreed with Smith but stated, "We have the utmost confidence in her loyalty to the work of reforming herself and others."

Georgie continued to use her wealth and knowledge to open up reform homes all over the country. She helped establish homes in Kalamazoo, Denver, Pittsburgh and Detroit and helped areas riddled with prostitution like Hurley, Wisconsin. When she ran out of money, she moved to Chicago for a bit and then married William Campbell of Superior, Wisconsin. She and her husband owned a vaudeville theater called the Gem Theater. Theaters didn't always have the best reputation, and some doubled as brothels, which sent rumors flying back home when she came back to the city eight years later in 1896 to defend her twin brother, Jared, who was being convicted of murder in Holland. (This story is featured in my book *Wicked Ottawa County, Michigan*.)

While the murder trial was exciting, reporters were just as pleased to talk to one of Grand Rapids' most famous prostitutes. When reporters interviewed her during her brother's trial, she didn't bother to hide who she had been. She didn't understand why they would even be interested in her former life of shame. She answered their questions, and they wrote that her "frankness" seemed to support her statement that she had never "backslid" into her former ways. "Georgie Young died eight years ago," she told the *Grand Rapids Press*, "and it does not seem fair that her ghost should rise up to haunt me. Since leaving Grand Rapids, I have lived another life."

One of the oldest men connected with the Grand Rapids Police Department, whose name was not mentioned, told the *Grand Rapids Press* that he was confident that Georgie had reformed if he had known her well enough. "No woman had ever conducted a disreputable house in Grand Rapids who gave the department so little trouble and she was as well known for her kind heart and philanthropic projects as her evil ways in other respects." Georgie eventually divorced from William and moved to Minneapolis, where she possibly became a nurse. She had one daughter with William named Connie, who went on to work and become an actress in the theater her father owned. Georgie passed away at the age of sixty-two in 1920. Her cremated remains were sent back to Grand Rapids to be buried with her mother in Oak Hill Cemetery.

Historically, Georgie was the most well-known scarlet sister of Grand Rapids because of her reform work and autobiography, but there were still plenty of other women who made their mark in the red-light districts of Grand Rapids.

ELLEN "NELLIE" SMITH

Nellie Smith had a career that spanned over a decade in the business. She was already showing up in early police blotters in 1878 as a proprietress. According to the *Grand Rapids Evening Leader*, she was "one of the best known members of the demi-monde." *Demimonde* was a French term describing women who were seekers of pleasure, wealth and the finer things in life. They lived their lives as if they were the upper class, even though they were not. One could say they were the upper class of the underworld. Nellie grew up on a farm in Plainfield Township and was considered pretty, very social and very popular with plenty of friends. Men always paid attention to her wherever she went. When she started working in Grand Rapids, she got a job at the Eagle Hotel. At some point, she entered the business, but it didn't appear that she was destitute. She married, but the marriage was short-lived, as her husband passed away.

When she began running her own house, Nellie quickly accrued property and increased her wealth. By 1881, city directories show her living on the infamous Kent Street, where she operated her house for six years until her death. Nellie passed away on July 13, 1887, at the age of forty-one after an illness. Her obituary said her lifestyle left her with a "serious impairment of her health" and that she hadn't been well for years, which could have been the remnants of a sexually transmitted disease or the result of too much drinking or drug use, such as opium or morphine.

The funeral was held two days later at her "gilded palace" on Kent Street on July 15. The *Grand Rapids Evening Leger* reported on the event and wrote, "The Magdalenes were sorrowful and solemn in the presence of death," and the funeral was largely attended by "the scarlet sisterhood." Men of high "social standing" were present, along with women from the Woman's Christian Temperance Union. Reverend J.E. Roberts of the Unitarian church conducted the funeral.

The general theme of his sermon was that if one led an "immoral life," it wasn't always because they were a bad person or enjoyed what they did.

"This woman who lies dead before us, if a little child would come crying to her door late on a stormy night, would take the waif in and tenderly care for it, while those who affect to look down upon those who have fallen would under such circumstances call for the patrol wagon. I am persuaded that those sentiments which make woman's life beautiful and lovely rise to high water mark in this woman's life," said the Reverend Roberts.

Tears were shed by everyone in the room. Before the beautiful coffin was closed forever, Nellie's sister cried out, "God bless you Ellen. I know you are in Heaven. I prayed for you…God blessed you and loved you and I know you are in Heaven." Anyone who had a dry eye started crying all over again after that. Nellie was buried by her own people, and her pallbearers were the biggest proprietresses in town: Georgie Young, Minnie Brown, Agnes Carpenter and Emma Rogers. She was laid to rest in Oak Hill Cemetery.

AGNES CARPENTER

Agnes was a longtime proprietress of a place known as "The Farm" that used to be at 86 McConnell Street. On August 7, 1874, she was acquitted by a jury after it declared her not guilty of running a house of ill repute, even though she did. The *Daily Democrat* wrote, "It is really astonishing what amount of evidence is required in a case of this kind to ensure a conviction, in fact it seems almost impossible to furnish proof enough to secure such a thing"— especially if you have the right people looking out for you in the political and higher social circles. Agnes was one of the well-liked proprietresses and didn't give the police too much grief, which is probably why her house existed for well over twenty-five years. She was born in England in 1839 and is listed in the Grand Rapids city directories as living on McConnell from 1876 to 1900, well into her sixties.

Many young girls got mixed up in the business when they innocently started to look for work to help out their families. They would respond to an ad in a paper looking for a domestic helper, and once they got the job, the whole thing would be turned around on them, tricking them into a life of prostitution. In July 1887, this happened to a young girl who was only fourteen. She went to work for a house on Wealthy Avenue, and then the mother found out her daughter was living at "The Farm." She had been duped into thinking she was getting an honest job and then brought into the home, probably by a procuress who had misled her.

This caused Agnes Carpenter's place to get raided by Superintendent Smith. Agnes had run her place by this time for over a decade. She was one of the well-known landowners and madams and was very wealthy. The police arrested three girls in the house and Agnes. One of the girls, Bessie Mason, was only fifteen and told the police that her mother had encouraged her to go into the business, as her mother was a "kept mistress." This wasn't the first time Agnes had been known to have younger girls in her house, and the *Grand Rapids Daily Democrat* wrote on July 9, 1887, "Agnes Carpenter has the reputation of being the most dangerous kind of a disreputable woman—a procuress."

Agnes was fined $28.50, which was much smaller than the normal fine. She told the judge that she did not "procure" Bessie Mason but found her sick and abandoned, so she took her in to give her shelter and get her well again. The *Grand Rapids Evening Leader* reported a completely opposite opinion of Agnes Carpenter. Her lawyer, Fred A. Maynard, reminded the paper that she had lived in Grand Rapids for over two decades, "owns a large amount of real estate and is a heavy tax payer and anyone who knows her life and deeds will tell you she is the best woman, the best hearted, most honest and kindest of that particular sort in the city. She keeps a house of ill-fame, I know, but it is a fact that can be proved that she has saved a great many young girls from lives of shame by her advice and counsel."

MOLLIE BOWEN

In July 1875, Mollie Bowen was in court for "keeping a house" on Waterloo Street. Neighbors watched from their windows and noticed the large number of men who went in and out of her house. The men would knock on the neighbors' doors, waking them up in the middle of the night, looking for "Mollie's place." The neighbors had had enough, and the police were told of the suspicious activity. Mollie was arrested and had a trial, but the jury was hung. There wasn't enough actual proof from witnesses that she was running a house of prostitution and not just a boardinghouse. There was plenty of word of mouth from people and gossip, and even police chief Moran seemed to be aware, but that wasn't enough to convict someone. The newspaper reporting on the incident sarcastically wondered "whether it could be successfully demonstrated to an average jury that the Grand Rapids & Indiana railroad depot was used as a depot."

Josephine Hamilton, a soiled dove, turned down a proposal of marriage from a man who knew her from her hometown of Niles. When she turned him down, he told her family about her "wicked life" in Grand Rapids, and disgusted and embarrassed, they cut off all communication with her. When her letters to family went unanswered, she became depressed and ashamed, and on February 7, 1879, Josephine killed herself with morphine. The house she had been working at was not run by a kind lady. The greedy woman took all of Josephine's clothing and possessions after she died; these could be resold to a new girl coming into the house who needed a few nice dresses to attract the men. The *Grand Rapids Eagle* noted the madam barely left Josephine with any clothes to be buried in.

Mollie Bowen heard what happened and stepped in and paid for clothing and the entire funeral. Many madams believed you took care of your own and stepped up when you could help. Georgie Young often paid for the funerals of her fellow fallen women. It was a sad life, and when one of the women took her own, the sadness of it held heavy on the hearts of the scarlet sisterhood. They knew how the hard lives they led destroyed many who could have had a chance if someone had given it to them.

SARAH GLOVER

Sarah Glover was the proprietress of a house on the infamous Kent Street. She left quite the impression on citizens. The *Grand Rapids Daily Eagle* wrote, "During her journeying about the city she rode a handsome black steed of considerable value." There is something charismatic about that image. Many of these proprietresses accrued a considerable amount of wealth during their time. Despite the obvious moral issues attached to the profession, they were essentially businesswomen in a time when women were not considered such. The *Daily Eagle* went on to say, "Her life has been one which is better untold, and she has taken with her to the grave secrets that will make many a man and some women breathe easier for knowing that she cannot reveal them." Madams typically kept a lot of secrets about people, often for a price. Higher-ups in the city would only visit high-end houses where they knew their identities would be kept secret. This not only gave the houses solid reputations but could also offer them immunity from the police.

A friend found Sarah's suicide letter sticking out from under her front door with a key to her house on December 2, 1887. The letter told the story of her life and how she wanted to be buried. Her body was found laying on her bed, "her eyes open and staring, and a pink froth which stood upon her bloodless lips." She was dressed in her riding clothes and expensive rings. This was what she wanted to be buried in. The coroner discovered a bottle that contained some sort of morphine mixture. Everywhere they looked, items in the house had notes attached to them telling the living who to give the item to. She had planned her death for some time. She was known to be addicted to early painkillers, known as anodynes and narcotics. Anodynes could be herbal in nature but would essentially dull the nervous system. It was reported she would dose herself and lay on her bed for hours in a seemingly catatonic state from the drugs.

She left other letters to people in the city, including one for Superintendent Israel Smith that was dated November 3, 1887, and began with, "I am tired of the life as you and others make it for me. I have nothing on earth for me. Nothing but misfortune has followed me since you took your office." She goes on to say in the letter that the police forcing her to move from the area had left her with no money and nowhere else to go.

The police during this period were aggressive in raiding houses of prostitution and wanted them moved or gone, and Sarah's place had been a main target. Prior to her death, the police were asking for a report on her moving status. She told them she'd get back to them with a "satisfactory answer," which was her suicide. Sarah didn't die poor by any standards of her day. Her bank account still had $1,508 in it, which is somewhere around $37,000 in today's currency.

The old newspapers contained dozens of other names with less information remembered. I will make it an ongoing research project through the years to continue to resurrect these fallen women in Michigan's history.

Bibliography

Mail-Order Murder

Cincinnati Post. "County Detective Watson." Tuesday, January 2, 1906.

Denver Post. "Man Who Admits Killing." Wednesday, October 4, 1916.

Denver Rocky Mountain News. "Aged Bluebeard Enacts Tragedy." Thursday, October 5, 1916.

Elkhart Truth. "Grand Rapids Slayer." Wednesday, October 4, 1916.

Elkhart Weekly Review. "Scott Mausell." Wednesday, January 3, 1906.

Grand Rapids Press. "Allen Laughs at Charge He Murdered Wife." Tuesday, October 3, 1916.

———. "Elkhart Clue May Identify Murder Victim." Monday, October 2, 1916.

———. "Mankind the Greatest Enigma." Thursday, October 5, 1916.

———. "Mausell Kindly Man, Says Wife." Friday, October 6, 1916.

———. "Mausell Left Death Trail." Monday, October 9, 1916.

———. "Mausell Sought to Lure Hoosier Woman." Friday, October 6, 1916.

———. "Members of Mausell Family Died." Wednesday, October 4, 1916.

———. "Murder Case Ably Handled by Officers." Thursday, October 5, 1916.

———. "Recalls Old Tragedy in Mausell's Family." Saturday, October 7, 1916.

————. "Scott Mausell Dies in Prison." Monday, August 4, 1919.

————. "Seek Mausell's Marriage Trail." Thursday, October 5, 1916.

————. "Suspect System for Murder of Brides." Wednesday, October 4, 1916.

————. "Wife-Slayer Begins Serving Life Term." Friday, October 6, 1916.

Sault Sainte Marie Evening News. "Alvah Mausell." Wednesday, November 16, 1904.

Wilkes-Barre Times. "New Year's Morning." Tuesday, January 2, 1906.

Notorious Clem Blood

Elkhart Daily Review. "State News." Friday, November 17, 1882.

Grand Rapids Press. "Admits Holdup Job." Thursday, October 20, 1910.

————. "Cora Blood Has Been Found." Friday, August 4, 1899.

————. "Grocer Murdered for His Money." Monday, September 26, 1910.

————. "Has Been Identified." Thursday, September 23, 1897.

————. "His Share Was But 10." Tuesday, October 18, 1910.

————. "Shellhorn's Time Commuted." Wednesday, October 4, 1916.

————. "Told by Their Heads." Friday, September 30, 1910.

————. "Were Only Friends." Thursday, September 23, 1897.

————. "Will End Lives at Marquette." Thursday, September 29, 1910.

Holland Evening Sentinel. "If Tom Davey…" Thursday, December 9, 1954.

Jackson Citizen Patriot. "Central City Brevities." Saturday, January 9, 1897.

————. "Changed Hands." Tuesday, November 19, 1889.

————. "Ex-Convict in Trouble." Tuesday, January 12, 1897.

————. "State News." Friday, September 24, 1897.

————. "Suicide at Grand Rapids." Friday, September 24, 1897.

Kalamazoo Daily Telegraph. "A Bad Man." Monday, March 27, 1893.

————. "Clem Blood." Wednesday, May 10, 1899.

————. "Juvenile Burglars." Wednesday, April 17, 1889.

Kalamazoo Gazette. "Attempted Murder." Sunday, January 10, 1897.

————. "Barred the Door." Friday, May 15, 1896.

————. "Blood on Trial." Friday, March 19, 1897.

————. "Blood Pleads Not Guilty." Saturday, January 14, 1905.

————. "Blood Sentenced." Friday, March 31, 1893.

————. "Body Is Identified." Thursday, September 23, 1897.

————. "Charged with Vagrancy." Friday, February 13, 1891.

———. "Clem Blood." Sunday, October 2, 1910.

———. "Clem Blood Again in County Jail." Wednesday, October 3, 1906.

———. "Clem Blood Given His Freedom Again." Friday, May 14, 1909.

———. "Clem Blood Uses Telephone." Saturday, December 22, 1906.

———. "Clem Took Poison." Wednesday, November 11, 1896.

———. "Concealed by Her Mother." Thursday, August 3, 1899.

———. "The Courts." Saturday, February 14, 1891.

———. "Deaths." Saturday, February 23, 1901.

———. "Did Clem Blood Send Blackhand Letter?" Saturday, May 1, 1909.

———. "Edward Blood." Tuesday, August 22, 1911.

———. "Ex-Convict on the Warpath." Friday, January 12, 1906.

———. "Funeral of Mrs. Blood." Sunday, February 5, 1905.

———. "Goes to the Reform." Saturday, January 21, 1905.

———. "He Left the Gang." Saturday, March 13, 1897.

———. "Jottings." Wednesday, January 18, 1893.

———. "Jottings." Saturday, July 15, 1893.

———. "Jottings." Saturday, November 20, 1897.

———. "Last of Clem Blood." Saturday, March 20, 1897.

———. "Local Gleanings." Friday, April 10, 1889.

———. "Loved Cherry Pie." Tuesday, March 28, 1893.

———. "More Jurors Drawn." Saturday, March 13, 1897.

———. "Officers Have Not Landed Blood." Friday, December 21, 1906.

———. "She Took Laudanum." Thursday, March 14, 1901.

———. "Shot the Sheriff." Saturday, January 9, 1897.

———. "Starts Life Sentence." Saturday, October 1, 1910.

———. "Taken to Industrial School." Thursday, May 4, 1905.

———. "Ten Long Years." Sunday, March 21, 1897.

———. "Thirty for Clem." Friday, October 12, 1906.

———. "Threat to Slay." Thursday, December 20, 1906.

———. "Twenty Years Ago." Saturday, July 25, 1908.

———. "Vern Blood." Friday, May 7, 1897.

———. "Vern Blood's Case." Saturday, February 6, 1897.

———. "Vern Blood's Crime." Thursday, January 14, 1897.

———. "Vernon Blood." Friday, January 14, 1897.

———. "Vern Sentenced." Thursday, February 11, 1897.

———. "Vern, Who Gave…" Wednesday, March 24, 1897.

———. "Wants Cash or Will Kill." Thursday, December 20, 1906.

———. "Woman Goes to Jail for Theft." Friday, January 13, 1905.

———. "Young Girl Arrested." Friday, January 20, 1905.

Saginaw News. "Cora, Ag 14…" Thursday, August 3, 1899.

————. "Michigan Dispatches." Friday, August 4, 1899.

Ypsilanti Commercial. "Clem Blood." Friday, April 14, 1893.

THE THOMSON JEWELRY STORE ROBBERY AND TRIPLE MURDER

Boston Herald. "Chip Robinson Buried at Old Home." Sunday, July 26, 1914.

————. "Inspector Is Murdered." Saturday, June 20, 1914.

————. "Robinson Kills Himself in Cell." Thursday, July 23, 1914.

————. "Robinson to Be Put on Trial." Tuesday, June 30, 1914.

Grand Rapids Press. "Bad Record of Two Years in Grand Rapids." Friday, September 19, 1913.

————. "Blackburn to Have a Police Court Hearing." Saturday, November 8, 1913.

————. "Blackburn Trial Is Soon to Be Staged." Friday, January 23, 1914.

————. "Boston Mob Frights to See Bandit." Monday, June 22, 1914.

————. "Chippy Robinson Pleads Not Guilty." Monday, June 22, 1914.

————. "Court Likens Murder Trial to Vaudeville." Thursday, February 6, 1914.

————. "Dangerous Trail Leads Halloran to Success." Saturday, June 20, 1914.

————. "Dead of Robinson Hastens Close." Wednesday, July 22, 1914.

————. "Fight in Three Courts to Get Ray Blackburn." Thursday, October 30, 1913.

————. "James Kendall Is Suspect." Monday, December 15, 1913.

————. "J.U. Smith Is a Witness for Ray Blackburn." Thursday, November 6, 1913.

————. "Lawrence Gives Warning." Tuesday, June 23, 1914.

————. "Lawrence Is Arraigned in Police Court." Saturday, April 18, 1914.

————. "Lawrence May Come Without Long Struggle." Wednesday, April 15, 1914.

————. "Lawrence Sells His Autograph on Train." Wednesday, July 29, 1914.

————. "Lawrence Soon Will Be Locked in Local Jail." Thursday, April 16, 1914.

————. "Lawrence to Be Sentenced." Monday, June 22, 1914.

————. "Murder and Confession." Saturday, June 20, 1914.

————. "No One Blamed for Thomson Murders." Thursday, October 16, 1913.

————. "Ray Blackburn Given Liberty." Saturday, March 28, 1914.

————. "Reward for Jewelry Store Murderers." Friday, September 19, 1913.

————. "Robinson Has Sick Wife." Wednesday, June 24, 1914.

————. "Robinson Indicted on Murder Charge." Tuesday, June 23, 1914.

————. "Second Man in Thomson Case Nabbed." Monday, June 16, 1914.

————. "Sentencing of Lawrence Last Act." Tuesday, July 28, 1914.

————. "Stolen Thomson Diamonds." Tuesday, April 14, 1914.

————. "Tattoo Marks Cover Jerry Thomas' Body." Friday, December 26, 1913.

————. "Theory Is Thomson Fired First Shot." Friday, September 19, 1913.

————. "Thomson's Diamonds Returned." Friday, July 31, 1914.

————. "Throng Fights for Sight of Ray Blackburn." Thursday, November 13, 1913.

————. "Tightening the Net." Friday, October 24, 1913.

————. "Toledo Sleuth Is Helping Halloran." Thursday, June 25, 1914.

————. "To Make Sure Identification of Blackburn." Friday, October 31, 1913.

————. "Townsend Dead." Monday, September 22, 1913.

————. "Townsend May Be the Third to Lose Life." Saturday, September 20, 1913.

————. "Two Identified as the Jewelry Store Gunmen." Thursday, October 23, 1913.

"The Thomson Murder Case." Kent County Michigan GenWeb Project. June 26, 2009. kent.migenweb.net.

THE JEALOUSY OF FRANK LOEFFLER

Flint Journal. "Murderer's Story." Wednesday, July 6, 1904.

Grand Rapids Herald. "Loeffler's Sanity." Thursday, July 7, 1904.

————. "Loeffler's Trunk." Friday, July 8, 1904.

————. "Make a Statement." Wednesday, July 27, 1904.

————. "Pretty Louisa Yakel Is Brutally Murdered." Tuesday, July 5, 1904.

————. "Sentence of Life." Saturday, July 9, 1904.

————. "Sets Up Insanity." Wednesday, July 6, 1904.

————. "Shot Her to Death." Tuesday, July 5, 1904.

————. "Story of a Brute." Monday, July 11, 1904.

————. "Story of Murder." Friday, July 8, 1904.

————. "Threats to Hang." Thursday, July 7, 1904.

————. "Wanted to Be Shot." Thursday, July 14, 1904.

Saginaw News. "Shoots Girl with Arm Around Neck." Tuesday, July 5, 1904.

Sault Ste. Marie Evening News. "Shot His Sweetheart." Wednesday, July 6, 1904.

West Side Advance. "Murder, He Wrote." Tuesday, February 28, 1989.

POTATO MASHER MURDER

Adrian Daily Telegram. "Accuses Husband of Brutal Murder." Friday, December 30, 1921.

Grand Rapids Herald. "Ethel Monroe Offers to Give Aid in Potato Masher Murder Case." Monday, December 19, 1921.

————. "Ethel Monroe to Help Police Solve Minnema Murder." Saturday, December 17, 1921.

————. "Police Seek Women to Solve Mystery of Masher Murder." Friday, December 16, 1921.

Grand Rapids Press. "Detective Doyle to Be Reinstated." Tuesday, January 17, 1922.

————. "Ethel Monroe to Help Police." Monday, December 19, 1921.

————. "Get New Theory in Minnema Case." Tuesday, December 20, 1921.

————. "Matthews Says He Did Not Murder and That He'll Be a Good Prisoner." Wednesday, January 4, 1922.

————. "Matthews to Be in Court Tuesday." Monday, January 2, 1922.

————. "Minnema Slayer Must Spend Life in State Prison." Tuesday, January 3, 1922.

————. "Potato Masher Used to Slay Lone Man." Friday, December 16, 1921.

————. "Scene of Murder." Friday, December 16, 1921.

————. "Stepson Quizzed in Minnema Case but Is Released." Saturday, December 17, 1921.

————. "Three Taken in Connection with Minnema Murder." Thursday, December 29, 1921.

————. "Toy Laden Auto Mystery Solved." Thursday, January 5, 1922.

Kalamazoo Gazette. "Blame Killing to Rum Quarrel." Saturday, December 17, 1921.

Muskegon Chronicle. "Woman Is Aide in Murder Sift." Monday, December 19, 1921.

Saginaw News. "Beneficiary Will Help Police Find G.R. Man's Slayer." Tuesday, December 20, 1921.

THE TRAGEDY OF CHARLIE POHLMAN

Grand Rapids Press. "Bullet in Brain: Mystery of Death of Little Charlie Pohlman, Was Not Killed by Cars." Monday, April 13, 1903.

————. "Full Story Told of Mystery of Death of Charlie Pohlman." Thursday, April 30, 1903.

————. "The Hasse Boys Crime." Thursday, April 30, 1903.

————. "Head Was Cut Off: Terrible Fate of Little Charlie Pohlman." Saturday, April 11, 1903.

————. "Killed in His Play by Boy Companions." Thursday, April 16, 1903.

————. "Mystery of Crime: How the Detectives Worked on Pohlman Case." Saturday, May 30, 1903.

————. "Mystery of Death: No Tangible Clue Yet Found in Pohlman Case." Tuesday, April 14, 1903.

————. "$100 Reward." Wednesday, April 15, 1903.

————. "Reward Is Offered in Pohlman Case." Wednesday, April 15, 1903.

————. "Seal Son's Lips: Detectives Complain of Action of Many Parents." Friday, April 17, 1903.

————. "Solved! Mystery of Death of Charlie Pohlman." Wednesday, April 29, 1903.

————. "Still in the Dark: Detectives Are Baffled in the Pohlman Case." Monday, April 20, 1903.

————. "Verdict! Furnishes No Key to Pohlman Tragedy." Saturday, April 18, 1903.

THE MYSTERIOUS DEATH OF MINA DEKKER

Grand Rapids Herald. "Chief Orders Man Detained for Quizzing." Wednesday, March 30, 1938.

———. "Free DeBlaey in Dekker Case." Sunday, March 13, 1938.

———. "Free Suspect After Dekker Case Quizzing." Wednesday, March 9, 1938.

———. "Friend Sought by Police in Dekker Girl's Murder." Monday, March 7, 1938.

———. "Peters Will Take Lie Detector Tests." Tuesday, March 15, 1938.

———. "Police Face 'Blind Alley' in Dekker Slaying." Sunday, March 6, 1938.

———. "Police Hold New Dekker Case Suspect." Wednesday, March 30, 1938.

———. "Police Hold Suspect in Dekker Slaying." Friday, March 11, 1938.

———. "Release Man Held for Murder Quiz." Thursday, March 31, 1938.

———. "Second Lie Test for Dekker Suspect." Thursday, March 10, 1938.

———. "Truth Serum Test for Man in Dekker Case." Saturday, March 12, 1938.

Grand Rapids Press. "Alibi Established for New Suspect." Thursday, March 31, 1938.

———. "Chief Spurs Probe into Girl's Murder." Tuesday, March 8, 1938.

———. "Dekker Murder: Still Unsolved." Thursday, March 4, 1948.

———. "Man Is Held in New Test by Detector." Friday, March 11, 1938.

———. "Slain Girl's Funeral Held." Monday, March 7, 1938.

———. "Slain Mina Dekker Took Secret Fear to Grave." Saturday, March 26, 1938.

———. "Suspect Detained in Girl Slaying." Wednesday, March 9, 1938.

———. "Ten Years Have Not Erased Dekker Family's Deep Sorrow." Thursday, March 4, 1948.

———. "Two Being Held in Dekker Case." Wednesday, March 30, 1938.

———. "Two Murders, Kidnap Case, Hanging Fire." Tuesday, March 16, 1938.

LaMarre, Virgil E. "Murder of the Beautiful Typist." *True Detective*, November 1938, 34–39.

Schock, David B., PhD. "Mina Dekker—Murder on the Third Floor." Delayed Justice. August 7, 2013. www.delayedjustice.com.

THE DAY HENRY BEDFORD WENT MAD

Aberdeen Daily News. "Michigan Justice." Monday, April 10, 1933.

Canton Repository. "Michigan Teacher, Slayer of 3, Ready to Begin Life Term." Sunday, April 9, 1933.

Grand Haven Daily Tribune. "Triple Slaying Is Admitted by G.R. Principal." Friday, April 7, 1933.

Grand Rapids Press. "Bedford Admits Triple Murder; Says Infatuation Impelled Him." Friday, April 7, 1933.

————. "Bedford's Educational Career Reveals He Has Moved Often as Student and an Instructor." Friday, April 7, 1933.

————. "School Principal Coldly Confesses Gruesome Crime." Friday, April 7, 1933.

Seattle Daily Times. "Teacher Admits He Killed Woman and 2 Children." Friday, April 7, 1933.

Tampa Tribune. "Husband Comes Home to Find Wife, and 2 Children Are Slain." Friday, April 7, 1933.

THE FIERY TEMPER OF DORA VELZY

Grand Rapids Press. "Blood in a Washbowl." Tuesday, June 13, 1893.

————. "Bloody Deed." Wednesday, June 7, 1893.

————. "Dora's Crime." Thursday, June 8, 1893.

————. "The Gray-Velzy Case." Saturday, June 10, 1893.

————. "Her Ammunition." Thursday, June 15, 1893.

————. "Scored the Police." Friday, June 9, 1893.

Jackson Citizen. "Dora Did the Deed." Thursday, June 15, 1893.

————. "Letters To Dora." Tuesday, June 13, 1893.

————. "A Woman's Revenge." Tuesday, June 13, 1893.

Kalamazoo Gazette. "All in Michigan." Saturday, June 10, 1893.

————. "Double Tragedy." Thursday, June 8, 1893.

Michigan Argus. "A Woman Scorned." Friday, June 16, 1893.

Muskegon Chronicle. "The Wages of Sin." Friday, June 9, 1893.

Saginaw News. "Murder and Suicide." June 8, 1893.

THE REFORMATION OF CLARA CONNOLLY

Flint Journal. "Connelly Returns to Her Husband." Friday, July 30, 1909.

Grand Rapids Press. "Attorney Still Busy: A.A. Ellis Seeks New Trial for Clara Connelly." Thursday, December 5, 1907.

———. "Begins New Life: Clara Connelly, Forgiven, Goes Back to Husband." Thursday, July 29, 1909.

———. "Crushed by Car." Tuesday, November 5, 1907.

———. "Goes to Detroit: Clara Connelly Is Sentenced by Judge Stuart." Thursday, December 12, 1907.

———. "Is Granted New Trial: Clara Connelly to Get Another Chance for Freedom." Tuesday, July 6, 1909.

———. "Jealous Man Is Killed by Woman." Thursday, August 15, 1907.

———. "New Trial Asked: Motion Is Filed in the Connelly Case." Saturday, November 22, 1907.

———. "Now Is a Free Woman: Clara Connelly Is Discharged by Judge Stuart." Saturday, November 12, 1910.

———. "Pleads Her Shame: Mrs. Connelly Says Husband Drove Her to Take His Life." Friday, August 16, 1907.

———. "Ready for Trial: Connelly Case to Be Taken Up on Nov. 18." Thursday, November 7, 1907.

———. "Tells of Shooting: Mrs. Clara Connelly on Stand in Superior Court." Tuesday, November 19, 1907.

———. "To a Higher Court Madeline Connelly, Alleged Murderess, Is Held." Tuesday, September 10, 1907.

———. "To Ask New Trial: Mrs. Connelly's Attorney Not Satisfied." Thursday, November 21, 1907.

———. "Woman Is Arraigned." Tuesday, October 22, 1907.

———. "Woman on Trial." Monday, November 18, 1907.

Kalamazoo Gazette. "Woman on Trial for Murder." Tuesday, November 19, 1907.

WHO KILLED JOSEPHINE OOM?

Flint Journal. "Effects of Bad Literature." Wednesday, November 22, 1905.

———. "Seals the Mystery: Coroner's Jury Gives Up in the Oom Murder Case." Friday, November 23, 1906.

Grand Rapids Press. "Another Clue Fails." Saturday, November 18, 1905.

———. "Are Hard at Work: Detection on Trail of the Oom Murderer." Monday, December 4, 1905.

———. "Asks for Chance: William Stegenga Says He Did Not Kill Josie Oom." Saturday, November 6, 1909.

———. "At Rest: Funeral of Josie Oom Held Today." Saturday, November 18, 1905.

———. "Family Is Remarkable: Take Their Bereavement with Calmness." Saturday, November 18, 1905.

———. "Inquest Is Quiet." Wednesday, January 10, 1906.

———. "Josie Oom Murder Is Still a Mystery." Thursday, November 16, 1905.

———. "Miss Oom Loved." Thursday, November 18, 1905.

———. "Mystery Is Deep." Saturday, November 25, 1905.

———. "No Clues to Work On, Police Baffled." Friday, January 17, 1913.

———. "Nothing Is Shown: Oom Inquest Develops No More Sensations." Wednesday, January 31, 1906.

———. "Oom Assassin Is Still a Free Man." Friday, November 17, 1905.

———. "Oom Case Inquest." Wednesday, December 27, 1905.

———. "Oom Inquest On." Friday, January 5, 1906.

———. "Panic Is Started." Wednesday, January 17, 1906.

———. "Reward Fund Is Raised: Citizens Anxious That Murderer Be Caught." Monday, November 20, 1905.

———. "Reward Growing: Capture of Josie Oom's Murderer Now Worth $950." Wednesday, November 22, 1905.

———. "Semeyn Her Lover." Friday, December 29, 1905.

———. "Stegenga Baffles: Marquette Prisoner Does Not Admit Oom Murder." Saturday, October 16, 1909.

———. "Two Hundred Dollars Reward." Friday, November 17, 1905.

———. "Was It a Woman? One Man Holds Murderer May Have Been a Female." Saturday, November 18, 1905.

———. "Was Wanton Murder." Thursday, November 16, 1905.

———. "Will Come Quick: Capture of Murderer Will Not Be a Slow Process." Saturday, November 18, 1905.

Muskegon Chronicle. "Looking for Boy; No Clue in Girl's Murder." Friday, November 17, 1905.

THE SCARLET SISTERHOOD OF GRAND RAPIDS

Baxter, Albert. *History of the City of Grand Rapids, Michigan*. New York: Munsell, 1891.

Evans, Hilary. *The Oldest Profession: An Illustrated History of Prostitution*. Newton Abbot: David & Charles, 1979.

Grand Rapids City Directories.

Grand Rapids Daily Democrat. "Acquitted." Saturday, August 8, 1874.

———. "Mollie Bowen." Friday, July 23, 1875.

———. "One More Unfortunate." Thursday, June 17, 1875.

———. "An Ordinance." Wednesday, July 7, 1875.

———. "Rescued from Shame." Saturday, July 9, 1887.

———. "An Unhappy Family." Tuesday, July 21, 1874.

Grand Rapids Daily Eagle. "About the Emerson." Monday, November 12, 1888.

———. "Added to the Library Fund." Saturday, August 31, 1878.

———. "Emerson Embroglio." Saturday, November 10, 1888.

———. "The Farm." Friday, September 5, 1873.

———. Friday, April 16, 1875.

———. "Margaret's Mistake." Wednesday, September 5, 1883.

———. "A Raid." Monday, November 7, 1881.

———. "Two of the Four." Monday, December 13, 1880.

———. "The Verdict." Friday, February 7, 1879.

Grand Rapids Daily Leader. "Correct Judge." Tuesday, March 2, 1880.

———. "House Kept by Ellen Smith." Monday, March 10, 1879.

Grand Rapids Daily Times. "Mother Carpenter's Bagnio." Tuesday, July 8, 1879.

Grand Rapids Evening Leader. "Another Raid." Wednesday, July 13, 1887.

———. "For Friendless Women." Friday, May 14, 1886.

———. "Frailty at a Funeral." Thursday, May 5, 1887.

———. "Kent Street Raid." Monday, June 27, 1887.

———. "Male Prostitutes Scored." Tuesday, July 1, 1884.

———. "The Municipal Dads." Tuesday, February 8, 1887.

———. "Nellie Smith." Friday, July 15, 1887.

———. "Probably Her Last Day." Tuesday, May 3, 1887.

———. "The Scarlet Sisters." Monday, July 11, 1887.

Grand Rapids Press. "Cases of Interest." Saturday, September 19, 1903.

———. "Closes the Dives." Saturday, October 3, 1903.

———. "Death Cheats Law." Saturday, March 19, 1910.

———. "For a Brother's Sake." Thursday, September 17, 1896.

―――. "Georgia Young." Monday, January 22, 1894.

―――. "Gives Women Week." Friday, December 6, 1912.

―――. "He Asked Delay." Monday, September 21, 1903.

―――. "He Loved Three." Friday, December 31, 1909.

―――. "Judge Is to Inquire." Friday, April 3, 1903.

―――. "Knew of the Place." Thursday, March 26, 1903.

―――. "Mate Morrison Gave Bail." Saturday, May 16, 1903.

―――. "Must Clean House." Friday, December 27, 1907.

―――. "Must Close Place." Monday, October 5, 1903.

―――. "Not a White Slave." Wednesday, January 19, 1910.

―――. "Not White Slave." Wednesday, January 12, 1910.

―――. "Saved by Grace." Thursday, July 27, 1893.

―――. "Some Old Streets." Saturday, May 6, 1905.

―――. "Warrant Now Out." Saturday, April 25, 1903.

―――. "Warrant to Issue." Friday, March 27, 1903.

―――. "Will Fight the Case." Monday, April 27, 1903.

Grand Rapids Saturday Evening Post. "The Revenge of the Outcast." Saturday, January 16, 1875.

―――. Saturday, July 31, 1875.

―――. "T.T. Will Smile." Saturday, September 3, 1881.

Grand Rapids Times. "Attempted Suicide." Friday, November 22, 1878.

Kalamazoo Gazette. "The Bethesda Home." Friday, January 1, 1890.

―――. "An Emerson Mystery." Friday, December 13, 1889.

―――. "The Reformation of Woman." Saturday, May 13, 1893.

Kneeland, George J. *Commercialized Prostitution in New York City*. New York: Century Co., 1913.

Jackson Citizen Patriot. "After Six Years." Friday, October 16, 1896.

Minneapolis City Directories.

Muskegon Chronicle. "Why Shield the Men?" Monday, March 3, 1919.

New York Tribune. "An Interesting Charity." Friday, November 29, 1889.

Rutter, Michael. *Upstairs Girls: Prostitution in the American West*. Helena, MT: Farcountry, 2005.

Superior, Wisconsin City Directories.

Telegram Herald. "The Dives." Sunday, June 5, 1887.

―――. "More Bad Houses." Monday, May 23, 1887.

―――. "Ourselves and the Others." Friday, May 20, 1887.

―――. "Reeking with Vice." Monday, May 16, 1887.

United State Census Records.

Young, Georgie. *A Magdalen's Life*. Grand Rapids, MI, 1889.

About the Author

Amberrose Hammond has been interested in the strange and unusual for as long as she's been on the planet. She is an avid local history enthusiast and enjoys getting others excited about Michigan's cool history. She is the author of *Ghosts & Legends of Michigan's West Coast* and *Wicked Ottawa County, Michigan.* Visit her at www.amberrosehammond.com.

Visit us at
www.historypress.net
....
This title is also available as an e-book